The Mirror of Relationship: Love, Sex and Chastity

A Selection of Passages
from the Teachings of
J. Krishnamurti

STUDY BOOK SERIES

A series of Study Books was conceived for use as concentrated study material on a particular topic. These books are an invaluable resource of excerpted material as they offer a sustained survey of each topic, allowing for a deeper comprehension of what Krishnamurti was conveying. Much of the material has been drawn from his works and the record of his public talks from 1933 to 1967. The following books have been published :

- **Action**
  [ISBN : 978-81-208-3273-2]
- **The Meditative Mind**
  [ISBN : 978-81-208-3272-5]
- **The Mirror of Relationship : Love, Sex and Chastity**
  [ISBN : 978-81-208-3274-9]
- **Individual & Society : The Bondage of Conditioning**
  [ISBN : 978-81-208-3275-6]
- **The Observer and the Observed**
  [ISBN : 978-81-208-3276-3]

Study Book Series

The Mirror of Relationship: Love, Sex and Chastity

A Selection of Passages
from the Teachings of
J. Krishnamurti

MOTILAL BANARSIDASS PUBLISHERS
PRIVATE LIMITED • DELHI

First Indian Edition : Delhi, 2012
First Published : USA, 1992

In Association With
KRISHNAMURTI FOUNDATION OF AMERICA
P.O. Box 1560, Ojai, California 93024 U.S.A
E-mail: kfa@kfa.org. Website: www.kfa.org

ISBN : 978-81-208-3274-9

Editors : DOUGLAS EVANS and ERODE STEEN

MOTILAL BANARSIDASS
41 U.A. Bungalow Road, Jawahar Nagar, Delhi 110 007
8 Mahalaxmi Chamber, 22 Bhulabhai Desai Road, Mumbai 400 026
203 Royapettah High Road, Mylapore, Chennai 600 004
236, 9th Main III Block, Jayanagar, Bangalore 560 011
Sanas Plaza, 1302 Baji Rao Road, Pune 411 002
8 Camac Street, Kolkata 700 017
Ashok Rajpath, Patna 800 004
Chowk, Varanasi 221 001

PRINTED AT INDIA
AND PUBLISHED BY NARENDRA PRAKASH JAIN FOR
MOTILAL BANARSIDASS PUBLISHERS PRIVATE LIMITED,
BUNGALOW ROAD, DELHI 110 007

Contents

Publisher's Note

The passages in this volume are taken from works by Krishnamurti. These include public talks, questions and answers, conversations, and writings.

Krishnamurti always spoke from such a large perspective that his whole vision was implied in any extended passage, or sometimes by even a very short quote. But if one wishes to see how a statement flows out of his whole discourse, one can find the context by referring to the source indicated with each extract. Doing so may be invaluable for deeper comprehension of the passages. With that in mind, a bibliography is provided at the end of the volume for your reference.

Introduction

Talking things over together as two friends . . .

In a few days we are going to have discussions, and we can start those discussions this morning. But if you assert and I assert, if you stick to your opinion, to your dogma, to your experience, to your knowledge, and I stick to mine, then there can be no real discussion because neither of us is free to inquire. To discuss is not to share our experiences with each other. There is no sharing at all; there is only the beauty of truth, which neither you nor I can possess. It is simply there.

To discuss intelligently, there must also be a quality not only of affection but of hesitation. You know, unless you hesitate, you can't inquire. Inquiry means hesitating, finding out for yourself, discovering step by step; and when you do that, then you need not follow anybody, you need not ask for correction or for confirmation of your discovery. But all this demands a great deal of intelligence and sensitivity.

By saying that, I hope I have not stopped you from asking questions! You know, this is like talking things over together as two friends. We are neither asserting nor seeking to dominate each other, but each is talking easily, affably, in an atmosphere of friendly companionship, trying to discover. And in that state of mind we do discover, but I assure you, what we discover has very little importance. The important thing is to discover, and after discovering, to keep going. It is detrimental to stay with what you have discovered, for then your mind is closed, finished. But if you die to what you have discovered the moment you have discovered it, then you can flow like the stream, like a river that has an abundance of water.

Saanen, 10th Public Talk, August 1, 1965
Collected Works, Vol. XV, p. 245

I. Life is a Movement in Relationship

We are together having a conversation. We are walking down a lane, wooded, with plenty of shadows and birds singing; we are sitting down together and talking about the whole problem of existence, which is very complex. We are not convincing each other about any subject, we are not trying to persuade each other, we are not trying to overcome the other through arguments or sticking dogmatically to one's own opinions, prejudices, but rather, together we are going to look at the world as it is and the world that is within us.

Many volumes have been written about the world outside of us—the environment, the society, politics, economics, and so on, but very few have gone to the very length of discovering what we actually are. Why human beings are behaving as they are doing—killing each other, constantly in trouble, following some authority or the other, some book, some person, some ideal, and having no right relationship with their friends, with their wives, with their husbands and with their children; why human beings have become, after so many millennia, so vulgar, so brutal, so utterly lacking in care, consideration, attention to others, and denying the whole process of what is considered love. Outwardly, man has lived with wars for thousands and thousands of years. We are now trying to stop nuclear war but we will never stop wars. There has been no demonstration throughout the world to stop wars, but there are demonstrations against particular wars, and these wars have been going on—people being exploited, oppressed and the oppressor becoming the oppressed. This is the cycle of human existence with sorrow, loneliness, a great sense of depression, the mounting anxiety, the utter lack of security. There is no relationship with society or with one's own intimate persons, a relationship in which there is no row, no conflict, quarrels, oppression, and so on. This is the world we live in, which I am sure you all know.

As we said yesterday, look at the activities of thought, because we live by thought. All our actions are based on thought, all our contemplated efforts are based on thought—our meditations, our worships, our prayer. Thought has brought about the division of nationalities which create wars, the division in religions as the Jew, as the Arab, the Muslim, the Christian, Hindu, Buddhist, and so on. Thought has divided the world not only geographically but also psychologically, inwardly. Man is fragmented, broken up not only at the psychological, mechanical level of his existence but also in his occupation. If you are a professor, you have your own small circle and live in that. If you are a businessman, you are in money making, or if you are a politician, you live within that area. And if you are a religious person, in the accepted sense of the word—doing various forms of *puja,* rituals, meditations, worshipping some idol, and so on—then also you live a fragmented life. Each fragment has its own energy, has its own capacity, has its own discipline, and each path plays an extraordinary role in contradicting the other path. You must know all this. This division—both outwardly, geographically, religiously, nationally, and the division that is between yourself and another—is such a waste of energy. It is a conflict: wasting our energy, quarrelling, dividing, each one pursuing his own thing, each one aspiring, demanding his own personal security, and so on.

All action takes energy, all thinking takes energy. This energy which is so constantly being broken up is a wastage of energy. When one energy contradicts another, one action contradicts another action—saying one thing and doing another, which is obviously a hypocritical acceptance of life—there is wastage of energy. All such activities must invariably condition the mind, the brain. We are conditioned as a Hindu, Buddhist, Muslim, Christian, with all the superstitions, beliefs. We are conditioned, and there is no question about it. There is no argument that we are not conditioned; we are—religiously, politically, geographically.

Until there is freedom from conditioning, freedom from the activities of thought which is creating great problems, those problems cannot possibly be solved. A new instrument is necessary to solve our human problems, and we are going to talk as we go along about it, but it is not for the speaker to tell you what the new quality of that instrument is; each one has to find for himself. That is why both of us must think together, if we can. That demands that both of us feel, enquire, search out, question, doubt, all these things that man has put together, all the things that we have created as barriers between each other. We as human beings living on this beautiful earth which is slowly being destroyed, living on this earth which is our earth—not the Indian earth or the British earth or the American earth—have to live intelligently, happily; but apparently, that is not possible because we are conditioned. This conditioning is like a computer: we are programmed; we are programmed to be Hindus, to be Muslims, to be Christians, Catholics, Protestants. For 2,000 years the Christian world has been programmed and the brain has been conditioned through that program, like the computer. So our brains are deeply conditioned and we are asking if it is at all possible to be free of that conditioning. Unless we are totally, completely, free of that limitation, mere enquiry or asking what is the new instrument which is not thought, has no meaning.

First, one must begin very near to go very far. We want to go so far without taking the first step, and perhaps the first step may be the last step. Are we understanding each other, are we communicating with each other, or am I talking to myself? If I am talking to myself, I can do this in my own room. But if *we* are talking, having a conversation together, that conversation has significance when both of us meet at the same level, with the same intensity, at the same time. That is love. That is the real, deep friendship. To me, this is not a lecture in the ordinary sense of the word. We are together trying to enquire and resolve human problems. That requires a great deal of enquiry because human problems are very, very complex. One must have the quality of patience, which is not of time. We are all impatient to get on—'tell me quickly something or other'—but if you have patience, that is, if you are not trying to achieve something, to arrive at some end, some goal, then enquire step by step into it.

As we said, we are programmed. Our human brain is a mechanical process. Our thought is a materialistic process, and that thought has been conditioned to think as a Buddhist, as a Hindu, as a Christian, and so on. So our brain is conditioned. Is it possible to be free from that conditioning? There are those who say it is not possible, because they ask, how can a brain which has been conditioned for so many centuries upon centuries, how can that conditioning be wiped away completely so that the human brain is extraordinarily pristine, original, capable of infinite capacity? Many people assert this, and are merely satisfied in modifying the conditioning. But we are saying that this conditioning can be examined, can be observed, and there can be total freedom from that conditioning. To discover for ourselves whether it is possible or not, we have to enquire into our relationship.

Relationship is the mirror in which we see ourselves as we are. All life is a movement in relationship. There is no living thing on earth which is not related to something or other. Even the hermit, a man who goes off to a lonely spot, is related to the past, is related to those who are around him. There is no escape from relationship. In that relationship which is the mirror in which we can see ourselves, we can discover what we are—

our reactions, our prejudices, our fears, depression, anxieties, loneliness, sorrow, pain, grief. We can also discover whether we love or there is no such thing as love. So, we will examine this question of relationship because that is the basis of love. That is the only thing we have now with each other. If you cannot find the right relationship, if you live your own particular narrow life apart from wife, husband, and so on, that isolated existence brings about its own destruction.

Relationship is the most extraordinarily important thing in life; if we don't understand that relationship, we cannot possibly create a new society. We are going to enquire very closely into what is relationship—why human beings throughout their long existence of life have never had a relationship in which there is neither oppression, possessiveness, attachment, contradiction, and so on. Why is there always this division—man, woman, we and they? We are going to examine together. This examination can be intellectual or merely verbal, but such intellectual comprehension has no value at all—it is just an idea, it is just a concept. But if you can look at your relationship as a whole, then perhaps you can see the depth and the beauty and the quality of relationship. Right, sir? Can we go on? We are asking, what actually is the present relationship with each other, not theoretical, not romantic, not idealistic, which are all unreal, but the actual, daily relationship of man, woman, with each other? Are we related at all? There is the biological relationship; our relationship is sexual, pleasurable. Our relationship is possessiveness, attachment, various forms of intrusion upon each other.

What is attachment? Why do we have such tremendous need for attachment? What are the implications of attachment? Why is one attached? When you are attached to anything, there is always fear in it, fear of losing it. There is always a sense of insecurity. Please observe it for yourself. There is always a sense of separation. I am attached to my wife. I am attached to her because she gives me pleasure sexually, gives me pleasure as a companion; you know all this, without my telling you. So, I am attached to her, which means I am jealous, frightened. Where there is jealousy, there is hatred. And is attachment love? That is one point to note in our relationship.

Then, in our relationship each one has, through the years, put together an image about the other. Those images she and he have created about each other is the actual relationship. They may sleep together, but the fact is that he and she have an image about each other, and in that relationship of images, how can there be any actual, factual, relationship with another? All of us from childhood have built images about ourselves and about others. We are asking a very, very serious question—can one live without a single image in our relationship? Surely, you all have an image about the speaker, haven't you? Obviously you have. Why? You don't know the speaker, actually you don't know. He sits on a platform, talks, but you have no relationship with him because you have an image about him. You have created an image about him, and you have your own personal images about yourself. You have got so many images about politicians, about businessmen, about the guru, about this and that. Can one live profoundly without a single image? Image may be conclusion about one's wife, image may be a picture, sexual picture, image may be some form of better relationship, and so on. Why do human beings have images at all? Please ask this question of yourself. When you have an image about another, that image gives you a sense of security.

Love is not thought. Love is not desire, love is not pleasure, love is not the movement of images, and as long as you have images about another, there is no love. And we ask, is it possible to live a life without a single image? Then you have a relationship with each other. As it is, it is like two parallel lines never meeting, except sexually. A man goes off to the office, ambitious, greedy, envious, trying to achieve a position in the business world, in the religious world, in the professional world, and the modern lady also goes off to the office, and they meet in their house to breed children. And then the whole problem of responsibility, problem of education, of total indifference, comes. It does not matter then what your children are, what happens to them. You want them to be like you—safely married, with a house, a job, etc. Right? This is our life, daily life, and it is really a sorrowful life. So, if one asks why human beings live by images—all your gods are images, the Christian god, the Muslim god and your god—you will see that they are created by thought, and thought is uncertain, fearful. There is no security in the things that thought has put together. Is it possible, then, to be free from our conditioning in our relationship? That is, to observe in the mirror of relationship attentively, closely, persistently, what our reactions are, whether they are mechanical, habitual, traditional. In that mirror you discover actually what you are. So, relationship is extraordinarily important.

We have to enquire into what it is to observe. How do you observe yourself, what you are, in the mirror of relationship? What does it mean to observe? This is really another important thing one has to find out. What does it mean to look? When you look at a tree, which is the most beautiful thing on the earth, one of the most lovely things on the earth, how do you look at it? Do you ever look at it, do you ever look at the new moon—the shape of the new moon, so delicate, so fresh, so young; have you ever looked at it? Can you look at it without using the word *moon*? Are you really interested in all this? I will go on like a river that goes on. You are sitting on the banks of the river looking at the river, but you don't become the river ever because you never take part of the river, you never join the beauty of the movement that has no beginning and no end.

So please consider what it is to observe. When you observe a tree, or a moon, something outside you, you always use the word—the tree, the moon; can you look at that moon, the tree, without naming it, without using the word to identify? Can you look without the word, without the content of the word, without identifying the word with the tree or the thing? Now, can you look at your wife, at your husband, at your children, without the word 'my wife', without an image? Have you ever tried it? When you observe without a word, without a name, without the form you have created about her or him, in that observation there is no center from which you observe. Then find out what happens. The word is thought. Thought is born out of memory. So you have the memory, the word, the thought, the image interfering between you and the other. Right? But here is no thought, thought in the sense, the word, the content of the word, the significance of the word to look, to observe. Then, in that observation, there is no center as 'me' looking at 'you'. Then only there is a right relationship with another. In that, there is a quality of learning, a quality of certain beauty, certain sensitivity.

Madras, India, December 26, 1982
Mind Without Measure, pp. 76-81

II. The Machinery of Image-Making

Have you ever looked at your wife, or your husband, or your children, or your neighbor, or your boss, or at any of the politicians? If you have, what is seen? The image you have about a person, the image you have about your politicians, the prime minister, your god, your wife, your children—that image is being looked at. And that image has been created through your relationship, or through your fears, or through your hopes. The sexual and other pleasures you have had with your wife, your husband, the anger, the flattery, the comfort, and all the things that your family life brings—a deadly life it is—have created an image about your wife or husband. With that image you look. Similarly, your wife or husband has an image about you. So the relationship between you and your wife or husband, between you and the politician is really the relationship between these two images. Right? That is a fact. How can two images which are the result of thought, of pleasure and so on, have any affection or love?

So the relationship between two individuals, very close together or very far, is a relationship of images, symbols, memories. And in that, how can there be real love? Do you understand the question?

New Delhi, 3rd Public Talk, December 22, 1966
Collected Works, Vol. XVII, pp. 112-13

To have relationship with another is only possible when there is no image.

Are we ever related to anyone, or is the relationship between two images which we have created about each other? I have an image about you, and you have an image about me. I have an image about you as my wife or husband, or whatever it is, and you an image about me also. The relationship is between these two images and nothing else. To have relationship with another is only possible when there is no image. When I can look at you and you can look at me without the image of memory, of insults and all the rest, then there is a relationship, but the very nature of the observer is the image, isn't it? My image observes your image—if it is possible to observe it—and this is called relationship, but it is between two images, a relationship which is nonexistent, because both are images. To be related means to be in contact. Contact must be something direct, not between two images. It requires a great deal of attention, an awareness, to look at another without the image which I have about that person, the image being my memories of that person—how he has insulted me, pleased me, given me pleasure, this or that. Only when there are no images between the two is there a relationship.

New York, 1st Public Talk, September 26, 1966
Collected Works, Vol. XVII, p. 7

To look there must be silence.

If you would look at a flower, any thought about that flower prevents your looking at it. The words *the rose, the violet, it is this flower, that flower, it is that species* keep you from observing. To look there must be no interference of the word, which is the objectifying of thought. There must be freedom from the word, and to look there must be silence; otherwise you can't look. If you look at your wife or husband, all the memories that you have had, either of pleasure or of pain, interfere with looking. It is only when you look without the image that there is a relationship. Your verbal image and the verbal image of the other have no relationship at all. They are nonexistent.

New York, 5th Public Talk, October 5, 1966
Collected Works, Vol. XVII, pp. 35-6

Why do we have images about ourselves?

To understand the full meaning of relationship with each other, however close, however distant, we must begin to understand why the brain creates images. We have images about ourselves and images about others. Why is it that each one has a peculiar image and identifies himself with that image? Is the image necessary, does it give one a sense of security? Does not the image bring about the separation of human beings?

We have to look closely at our relationship with wife, husband or friend; look very closely, not trying to avoid it, not trying to brush it aside. We must together examine and find out why human beings throughout the world have this extraordinary machinery that creates images, symbols, patterns. Is it because in those patterns, symbols and images, great security is found?

If you observe you will see that you have an image about yourself, either an image of conceit which is arrogant, or the contrary to that. Or you have accumulated a great deal of experience, acquired a great deal of knowledge, which in itself creates the image, the image of the expert. Why do we have images about ourselves? Those images separate people. If you have an image of yourself as Swiss or British or French and so on, that image not only distorts your observation of humanity but it also separates you from others. And wherever there is separation, division, there must be conflict—as there is conflict going on all over the world, the Arab against the Israeli, the Muslim against the Hindu, one Christian church against another. National division and economic division, all result from images, concepts, ideas, and the brain clings to these images—why? Is it because of our education, because of our culture in which the individual is most important and where the collective society is something totally different from the individual? That is part of our culture, part of our religious training and of our daily education. When one has an image about oneself as being British or American, that image gives one a certain security. That is fairly obvious. Having created the image about oneself that image becomes semi-permanent; behind that image, or in that image, one tries to find security, safety, a form of resistance. When one is related to another, however delicately, however subtly, psychically or physically, there is a response based on an image. If one is married or related intimately with somebody, an image is formed in one's daily life; whether one is acquainted for a week or ten years, the image is slowly formed about the other person step by step; every reaction is remembered, adding to the image and stored up in the brain so that the relationship—it may be physical, sexual, or psychical—is actually between two images, one's own and the other's.

The speaker is not saying something extravagant, or exotic, or fantastic, he is merely pointing out that these images exist. These images exist and one can never know another completely. If one is married or one has a girlfriend, one can never know her completely; one thinks one knows her because having lived with that person one has accumulated memories of various incidents various irritations and all the occurrences which happen in daily life; and she also has experienced her reactions and their images are established in her brain. Those images play an extraordinarily important part in one's life. Apparently very few of us are free from any form of image. The freedom from images is real freedom. In that freedom there is no division brought about by images. If one is a Hindu, born in India with all the conditioning to which one is subject, the conditioning of the race, or of a particular group with its superstitions, with its religious beliefs, dogmas, rituals—the whole structure of that society—one lives with that complex of images, which is one's conditioning. And however much one may talk about brotherhood, unity, wholeness, it is merely empty words having no actual daily meaning. But if one frees oneself from all that imposition, all the conditioning of all that superstitious nonsense, then one is breaking down the image. And also in one's relationship, if one is married or lives with somebody, is it possible not to create an image at all—not to record an incident which may be pleasurable or painful, in that particular relationship, not to record either the insult or the flattery, the encouragement or discouragement?

Is it possible not to record at all? Because if the brain is constantly recording everything that is happening, psychologically, then it is never free to be quiet, it can never be tranquil, peaceful. If the machinery of the brain is operating all the time it wears itself out. This is obvious. It is what happens in our relationships with each other—whatever the relationship is—and if there is constant recording of everything then the brain slowly begins to wither away and that is essentially old age.

So, in investigating we come upon this question: is it possible in our relationships, with all their reactions and subtleties, with all their essential responses, is there a possibility of not remembering? This remembering and recording is going on all the time. We are asking whether it is possible not to record psychologically, but only to record that which is absolutely necessary? In certain directions it is necessary to record. For example, one must record all that which is necessary to learn mathematics. If I am to be an engineer I must record all the mathematics related to structures, and so on. If I am to be a physicist I must record that which has already been established in that subject. To learn to drive a car I must record. But is it necessary in our relationships to record, psychologically, inwardly, at all?

The remembrance of incidents past, is that love? When I say to my wife, 'I love you,' is that from a remembrance of all the things we have been through together—the incidents, the travail, the struggles—which are recorded, stored in the brain? Is that remembrance actual love?

So, is it possible to be free and not to record psychologically at all? It is only possible when there is complete attention. When there is complete attention there is no recording.

I do not know why we want explanations, or why it is that our brains are not swift enough to capture, to have an insight into, the whole thing immediately. Why is it that we cannot see this thing, the truth of all this, and let that truth operate and therefore cleanse the slate and have a brain that is not recording at all psychologically? But most human beings are rather sluggish, they rather like to live in their old patterns, in their particular habits of thought; anything new they reject because they think it is much better to live with the known rather than with the unknown. In the known there is safety—at least they think there is safety, security—so they keep on repeating, working and struggling within that field of the known. Can we observe without the whole process and machinery of memory operating?

Saanen, Switzerland, July 19, 1981
The Network of Thought, pp. 40-3

To establish right relationship is to destroy the image.

There is no love between two images. How can I love you and you love me, if you have an image about me, if you have ideas about me? If I have hurt you, if I have pushed you, if I have been ambitious, clever, and gone ahead of you, how can you love me? How can I love you if you threaten my position, my job, if you run away with my wife? If you belong to one country and I to another, if you belong to one sect—Hinduism or Buddhism or

Catholicism and the rest of it—and I am a Muslim, how can we love each other? So unless there is a radical transformation in relationship, there cannot possibly be peace. By becoming a monk or a *sannyasi* and running away to the hills, you are not going to solve your problems, because wherever you live, whether in a monastery or in a cave or in a mountain, you are related. You cannot possibly isolate yourself either from your own image which you have created about God, about truth, or from your own image about your own self and all the rest of it.

So, to establish right relationship is to destroy the image. Do you understand what it means to destroy the image? It means to destroy the image about yourself—that you are a Hindu; that I am a Pakistani, a Muslim, a Catholic, a Jew, or a communist and so on. You have to destroy the machinery that creates the image—the machinery that is in you and the machinery that is in the other; otherwise, you may destroy one image and the machinery will create another image. So, one has not only to find out the existence of the image—that is, to be aware of your particular image—but also to be aware of what the machinery is that creates the image.

Now, let us see what that machinery is. You understand my question? That is, first one has to be conscious, to be aware, to know—not verbally, not intellectually, but actually know as a fact—the existence of this image. It is one of the most difficult things, because to know the image implies a great deal. You can know, you can observe that microphone—that is a fact. You may call it by different names, but if we understand what you call by these names, then we see the fact of it. So there is no interpretation there; we both know it is a microphone. But it is a different thing to understand the image without interpretation, to see the fact of that image without the observer, because the observer is the image-maker and the image is the thought of the observer. This is a very complex thing. You cannot just say, "I will destroy the image," and meditate about it, or do some kind of trick, or hypnotize yourself that you can destroy the image—it is not possible. It requires tremendous understanding. It requires great attention and exploration, not a conclusion at any time; a man that is exploring can never come to a conclusion. And life is an immense river that is flowing, moving incessantly. Unless you follow it freely, with delight, with sensitivity, with great joy, you will not see the full beauty, the volume, the quality of that river. So we must understand this problem.

When we use the word *understand,* we mean by that word, don't we: not intellectually. Perhaps you have understood the word *image,* how it is created by knowledge, by experience, by tradition, by the various strains and stresses in family life, work in the office, the insults—all that makes up the image. What is the machinery that makes that image? You understand? The image must be put together. The image must be maintained; otherwise it will collapse. So you must find out for yourself how this machinery works. And when you understand the nature of the machinery and the significance of that machinery, then the image itself ceases to be—the image—not only the conscious image, the image that you have of yourself consciously and are aware of superficially, but also the image deep down, the whole of it. I hope I am making this thing clear.

One has to go into and find out how the image comes into being and if it is possible to stop the machinery that creates it. Then only is there a relationship between human beings— it will not be between two images, which are dead entities. It is very simple. You flatter me, you respect me; and I have an image about you, through insult, through flattery. I have experience—pain, death, misery, conflict, hunger, loneliness. All that creates an image in me; I am that image. Not that I am the image, not that the image and me are different; but the 'me' is that image; the thinker is that image. It is the thinker that creates the image. Through his responses, through his reactions—physical, psychological, intellectual and so on—the thinker, the observer, the experiencer, creates that image through memory, through thought. So, the machinery is thinking, the machinery comes into existence through thought. And thought is necessary, otherwise you cannot exist.

So, first see the problem. Thought creates the thinker. The thinker begins to create the image about himself: he is the atma, he is God, he is the soul, he is a Brahmin, he is a non-Brahmin, he is a Muslim, he is a Hindu and the rest of it. He creates the image and he lives in it. So thinking is the beginning of this machinery. And you will say, "How can I stop thinking?" You cannot. But one can think and not create the image; one can observe that one is a communist or a Muslim. You can observe this, but why should you create an image about yourself? You only create an image about me as a Muslim, as a communist or whatever it is, because you have an image about yourself, which judges me. But if you had no image about yourself, then you would look at me, observe me, without creating the image about me. That is why this requires a great deal of attention, a great deal of observation of your own thoughts, feelings.

So one begins to see that most of our relationship is actually based on this image-formation, and having formed the image, one establishes or hopes to establish relationship between two images. And naturally there is no relationship between images. If you have an opinion about me and if I have an opinion about you, how can we have any relationship? Relationship exists only when it is free, when there is freedom from this image-formation—we will go into this during the talks that come. Only when this image is broken up and the image-formation ceases, will there be the ending of conflict, the total ending of conflict. Then only will there be peace, not only inwardly, but also outwardly. It is only when you have established that peace inwardly that the mind, being free, can go very far.

You know, sir, freedom can only exist when the mind is not in conflict. Most of us are in conflict, unless we are dead. You hypnotize yourself, or identify yourself with some cause, some commitment, some philosophy, some sect, or some belief—you are so identified that you are just mesmerized, and you live in a state of sleep. Most of us are in conflict; the ending of that conflict is freedom. With conflict you cannot have freedom. You may seek, you may want it; but you can never have it.

So, relationship means the ending of the machinery which puts together the image, and with the ending of that machinery, right relationship is established; therefore, there is the ending of conflict. And when there is the end of conflict, there is freedom, obviously—actual freedom, not as an idea, but the actual state as a fact. Then, in that state of freedom, the mind, which is no longer twisted, no longer tortured, which is not biased, which is not given to any fancy, any illusion, any mystical conception, or vision—that mind can go very far. Far, not in time or space, because there is no space and time, when there is freedom. I am using the words *very far* in the sense that then we can discover—these are words which really have no meaning—then in that freedom there is a state of emptiness, a state of joy, a bliss which no God, no religion, no book can give you.

That is why unless this relationship is established between you and your wife, your neighbor, your society, between you and other people, you will never have peace and therefore no freedom. And as a human being, not as an individual, you can then transform society. Not the socialist, not the communist—nobody will do it. Only the man that has understood what right relationship is—only such a man can bring about a society in which a human being can live without conflict.

Bombay, 1st Public Talk, February 13, 1966
Collected Works, Vol. XVI, pp. 45-7

The moment I am not paying attention, thought . . . takes over and creates the image.

Questioner: For the making of images to end, must thought also end? Is one necessarily implied in the other? Is the end of image-making really a foundation upon which one can begin to discover what love and truth are? Or is that ending the very essence of truth and love?

KRISHNAMURTI: We live by the images created by the mind, by thought. These images are continuously added and taken away. You have your own image about yourself; if you are a writer you have an image about yourself as a writer; if you are a wife or a husband, each has created an image about himself or herself. This begins from childhood, through comparison, through suggestion, by being told you must be as good as the other chap, or you must not do, or you must; so gradually this process accumulates. And in our relationships, personal and otherwise, there is always an image. As long as the image exists, you are liable to be either wounded, bruised, or hurt. And this image prevents there being any actual relationship with another.

Now the questioner asks: Can this ever end, or is it something with which we have to live everlastingly? And he also asks: In the very ending of the image, does thought end? Are they inter-related, image and thought? When the image-making machinery comes to an end, is that the very essence of love and truth?

Have you ever actually ended an image—voluntarily, easily, without any compulsion, without any motive? Not, "I must end the image I have of myself, I will not be hurt." Take one image and go into it; in going into it, you discover the whole movement of image-making. In that image you begin to discover there is fear, anxiety; there is a sense of isolation; and if you are frightened you say, "Much better keep to something I know than something I do not know." But if you go into it fairly seriously and deeply, you enquire as to who or what is the maker of this image, not one particular image but image-making as a whole. Is it thought? Is it the natural response, natural reaction, to protect oneself physically and psychologically? One can understand the natural response to physical protection, how to have food, to have shelter, to have clothes, to avoid being run over by a bus, and so on. That is a natural, healthy, intelligent response; in that there is no image. But psychologically, inwardly, we have created this image which is the outcome of a series of incidents, accidents, hurts, irritations.

Is this psychological image-making the movement of thought? We know that thought does not, perhaps to a very large degree, enter into the self-protective physical reaction. But the psychological image-making is the outcome of constant inattention which is the very essence of thought. Thought in itself is inattentive. Attention has no center, it has no point from which to go to another point, as in concentration. When there is complete attention there is no movement of thought. It is only to the mind that is inattentive that thought arises.

Thought is matter; thought is the outcome of memory; memory is the outcome of experience, and that must always be limited, partial. Memory, knowledge can never be complete, they are always partial, therefore inattentive.

So when there is attention there is no image-making, there is no conflict; you see the fact. If when you insult me or flatter me and I am completely attentive, then it does not mean a thing. But the moment I am not paying attention, thought, which is inattentive in itself, takes over and creates the image.

Now, the questioner asks: Is the ending of image-making the essence of truth and love? Not quite. Is desire love? Is pleasure love? Most of our life is directed towards pleasure in different forms, and when that movement of pleasure, sex, etc., takes place we call that love. Can there be love when there is conflict, when the mind is crippled with problems, problems of heaven, problems of meditation, problems between man and woman? When the mind is living in problems, which most of our minds are, can there be love?

Can there be love when there is great suffering, physiological as well as psychological? Is truth a matter of conclusion, a matter of opinion, of philosophers, of theologians, of those who believe so deeply in dogma and ritual, which are all man-made? Can a mind so conditioned know what truth is? Truth can only be when the mind is totally free of all this jumble. Philosophers and others never look at their own lives; they go off into some metaphysical or psychological world, about which they begin to write and publish and become famous. Truth is something that demands extraordinary clarity of mind, a mind that has no problem whatsoever, physical or psychological, a mind that does not know conflict. Even the memory of conflict must end. With the burden of memory we cannot find truth. It is impossible. Truth can only come to a mind that is astonishingly free from all that is man-made.

Those are not words to me, you understand? If it was not something actual, I would not speak, I would be dishonest to myself. If it were not a fact I would be such a terrible hypocrite. This requires tremendous integrity.

Questions and Answers, pp. 31-3

III. Understanding Pleasure and Desire

We are seeking pleasure, and we want all relationship to be based on it.

One has to understand relationship, because that is life. We can't exist without relationship of some kind. You can't withdraw into isolation, build a wall around yourself, as most people do, because that act of living in a sheltered, secure, isolated state of resistance only breeds more confusion, more problems, more misery. Life is, if one observes, a movement in action, a movement in relationship, and that is our whole problem: How to live in this world, where relationship is the very basis of all existence; how to live in this world so that relationship doesn't become monotonous, dull, something that is ugly, repetitive.

Our minds do conform to the pattern of pleasure—and life is not mere pleasure, obviously. But we want pleasure. That is the only thing we are really seeking deeply, inwardly, secretly. We try to get pleasure out of almost anything, and pleasure, if one observes, not only isolates and confuses the mind, but it also creates values which are not true, not actual. So pleasure brings illusion. A mind that is seeking pleasure, as most of us are, not only isolates itself, but must invariably be in a state of contradiction in all its relationships, whether it is the relationship with ideas, with people, or with property; it must always be in conflict. So that is one of the things one has to understand: that our search in life is fundamentally the demand, the urge, the seeking of pleasure.

Now, this is very difficult to understand because, why shouldn't one have pleasure? You see a beautiful sunset, a lovely tree, a river that has a wide, curving movement, or a beautiful face, and to look at it gives great pleasure, delight. What is wrong with that? It seems to me the confusion and the misery begin when that face, that river, that cloud, that mountain, becomes a memory, and this memory then demands a greater continuity of pleasure; we want such things repeated. We all know this. I have had a certain pleasure, or you have had a certain delight in something, and we want it repeated. Whether it be sexual, artistic, intellectual, or something not quite of this character, we want it repeated—and I think that is where pleasure begins to darken the mind and create values which are false, not actual.

What matters is to understand pleasure, not try to get rid of it—that is too stupid. Nobody can get rid of pleasure. But to understand the nature and the structure of pleasure, is essential; because if life is only pleasure, and if that is what one wants, then with pleasure go the misery, the confusion, the illusions, the false values which we create, and therefore there is no clarity. It is a simple fact, psychologically as well as biologically, that we are seeking pleasure, and we want all relationship to be based on it; and hence, when relationship is not pleasurable, there is a contradiction, and then the conflict, the misery, the confusion, and the agony begin.

Paris, 3rd Public Talk, May 23, 1965
Collected Works, Vol. XV, pp. 163-4

Pleasure is the continuation and the cultivation in thought of a perception.

What is the significance and the meaning of pleasure, which every human being is seeking and pursuing at any cost? What is pleasure? There is the pleasure derived from possessions; the pleasure derived from a capacity or talent; the pleasure when you dominate another; the pleasure of having tremendous power, politically, religiously or economically; the pleasure of sex; the pleasure of the great sense of freedom that money gives. There are multiple forms of pleasure. In pleasure there is enjoyment, and further on there is ecstasy, the taking delight in something and the sense of ecstasy. "Ecstasy" is to be beyond yourself. There is no self to enjoy. The self—that is the me, the ego, the personality—has all totally disappeared, there is only that sense of being outside. That is ecstasy. But that ecstasy has nothing whatsoever to do with pleasure.

You take a delight in something; the delight that comes naturally when you look at something very beautiful. At that moment, at that second, there is neither pleasure, nor joy, there is only that sense of observation. In that observation the self is not. When you look at a mountain with its snow cap, with its valleys, its grandeur and magnificence, all thought is driven away. There it is, that greatness in front of you and there is delight. Then thought comes along registering as memory what a marvellous and lovely experience it was. Then that registration, that memory, is cultivated and that cultivation becomes pleasure. Whenever thought interferes with the sense of beauty, the sense of the greatness of anything, a piece of poetry, a sheet of water, or a lonely tree in a field, it is registration. But, to see it and not register it—that is important. The moment you register it, the beauty of it, then that very registration sets thought into action; then the desire to pursue that beauty, which becomes the pursuit of pleasure. One sees a beautiful woman, or man; instantly it is registered in the brain;

then that very registration sets thought into motion and you want to be in her or his company and all that follows. Pleasure is the continuation and the cultivation in thought of a perception. You have had sexual experience last night, or two weeks ago, you remember it and desire the repetition of it, which is the demand for pleasure.

Is it possible to register only the things that are absolutely necessary? The necessary things are the knowledge of how to drive a car, how to speak a language, technological knowledge, the knowledge of reading, writing and so on. But in our human relationships, those between man and woman for example, every incident in that relationship is registered. What takes place? The woman is irritated, nags, or is friendly, kindly, or says something just before the man goes off to the office, which is ugly; so from this there is built up, through registration, an image about her and she builds an image about him—this is factual. In human relationships, between man and woman, or between neighbors and so on, there is registration and the process of image making. But when the husband says something ugly listen to it carefully, end it, do not carry it on; then you will find that there is no image-making at all. If there is no image-making between a man and a woman the relationship is entirely different; there is no longer the relationship of one thought opposed to another thought—which is called relationship, which actually it is not; it is just ideas.

Pleasure follows registration of an incident in the continuation given by thought. Thought is the root of pleasure. If you had no thought and you saw a beautiful thing it would rest at that. But thought says: "No, I must have that"; from this flows the whole movement of thought.

What is the relationship of pleasure to joy? Joy comes to you uninvited, it happens. You are walking along in a street, or sitting in a bus, or wandering in the woods, seeing the flowers, the hills, and the clouds and the blue sky and suddenly there is the extraordinary feeling of great joy; then comes the registration, thought says: "What a marvellous thing that was, I must have more of it." So, again, joy is made into pleasure by thought. This is seeing things as they are, not as you want them to be; it is seeing them exactly, without any distortion, seeing what is taking place.

What is love? Is it pleasure; which is the continuation of an incident through the movement of thought? Is the movement of thought love? Is love remembrance? A thing has happened and living in its remembrance, feeling that remembrance of something which is over, resuscitating it and saying, "What a marvellous thing that was when we were together under that tree; that was love"—all that is the remembrance of a thing that is gone. Is that love? Is love the pleasure of sex?—in which there is tenderness, kindliness and so on—is that love? That is not to say that it is, or that it is not.

We are questioning everything that man has put together of which he says: "This is love." If love is pleasure then it gives emphasis to the remembrance of past things and therefore brings about the importance of the me—my pleasure, my excitement, my remembrances. Is that love? And is love desire? What is desire? One desires a car; one desires a house; one desires prominence, power, position. There are infinite things one desires: to be as beautiful as you are, to be as intelligent, as clever, as smart as you are. Does desire bring clarity?

The thing that is called love is based on desire—desire to sleep with a woman, or sleep with a man, desire to possess her, dominate her, control her: "She is mine, not yours." Is love in the pleasure derived in that possession, in that dominance? Man dominates the world and now there is woman fighting the domination.

What is desire? Does desire bring about clarity? In its field does compassion flower? If it does not bring clarity and if desire is not the field in which the beauty and the greatness of compassion flower, then what place has desire? How does desire arise?

One sees a beautiful woman, or a beautiful man—one sees. There is the perception, the seeing, then the contact, then the sensation, then that sensation is taken over by thought, which becomes the image with its desire. You see a beautiful vase, a beautiful sculpture—ancient Egyptian, or Greek—and you look at it and you touch it; you see the depth of sculpture of the figure sitting cross-legged. From that there is a sensation. What a marvellous thing and from that sensation desire; "I wish I had that in my room; to look at it every day, touch it every day"—the pride of possession, to have such a marvellous thing as that. That is desire: seeing, contact, sensation, then thought using that sensation to cultivate the desire to possess—or not to possess.

Now comes the difficulty: realizing this the religious people have said: "Take vows of celibacy; do not look at a woman; if you do look treat her as your sister, mother, whatever you like; because you are in the service of God you need all your energy to serve Him; in the service of God you are going to have great tribulations, therefore be prepared, but do not waste your energy." But the thing is boiling and we are trying to understand that desire which is constantly boiling, wanting to fulfill, wanting to complete itself.

Desire arises from the movement: seeing–contact–sensation–thought with its image–desire. Now we are saying: seeing–touching–sensation, that is normal, healthy—end it there, do not let thought take it over and make it into a desire. Understand this and then you will also understand that there will be no suppression of desire. You see a beautiful house, well proportioned with lovely windows, a roof that melts into the sky, walls that are thick and part of the earth, a beautiful garden, well kept. You look at it, there is sensation; you touch it—you may not actually touch it but you touch it with your eyes—you smell the air, the herbs, the newly-cut grass. Can you not end it there? End it there, say: "It is a beautiful house"; but there is no registration and no thought which says: "I wish I had that house"—which is desire and the continuation of desire. You can do this so easily; and I mean easily, if you understand the nature of thought and desire.

The Wholeness of Life, pp. 167-71

To understand desire is to be choicelessly aware of its movements.

Desire is energy, and it has to be understood; it cannot merely be suppressed, or made to conform. Any effort to coerce or discipline desire makes for conflict, which brings with it insensitivity. All the intricate ways of desire must be known and understood. You cannot be taught and you cannot learn the ways of desire. To understand desire is to be choicelessly aware of its movements. If you destroy desire, you destroy sensitivity, as well as the intensity that is essential for the understanding of truth.

Commentaries on Living, Series III, p. 294

What is the source of desire?

When we say we love another, in that love there is desire, the pleasurable projections of the various activities of thought. One has to find out whether love is desire, whether love is pleasure, whether in love there is fear; for where there is fear there must be hatred, jealousy, anxiety, possessiveness, domination. There is beauty in relationship and the whole cosmos is a movement in relationship. Cosmos is order and when one has order in oneself one has order in one's relationships and therefore the possibility of order in our society. If one enquires into the nature of relationship one finds it is absolutely necessary to have order, and out of that order comes love.

What is beauty? You see the fresh snow on the mountains this morning, clean, a lovely sight. You see those solitary trees standing black against that white. Looking at the world about us you see the marvellous machinery, the extraordinary computer with its special beauty; you see the beauty of a face, the beauty of a painting, beauty of a poem—you seem to recognize beauty out there. In the museums or when you go to a concert and listen to Beethoven, or Mozart, there is great beauty—but always out there. In the hills, in the valleys with their running waters, and the flight of birds and the singing of a blackbird in the early morning, there is beauty. But is beauty only out there? Or is beauty something that only exists when the 'me' is not? When you look at those mountains on a sunny morning, sparkling clear against the blue sky, their very majesty drives away all the accumulated memories of yourself—for a moment. There the outward beauty, the outward magnificence, the majesty and the strength of the mountains, wipes away all your problems—if only for a second. You have forgotten yourself. When there is total absence of yourself beauty is. But we are not free of ourselves; we are selfish people, concerned with ourselves, with our importance or with our problems, with our agonies, sorrows, and loneliness. Out of desperate loneliness we want identification with something or other and we cling to an idea, to a belief, to a person, especially to a person. In dependency all our problems arise. Where there is psychological dependency, fear begins. When you are tied to something corruption begins.

Desire is the most urgent and vital drive in our life. We are talking about desire itself, not desire for a particular thing. All religions have said that if you want to serve God you must subjugate desire, destroy desire, control desire. All the religions have said: substitute for desire an image that thought has created—the image that the Christians have, that the Hindus have and so on. Substitute an image for the actual. The actual is desire—the burning of it and they think that one can overcome that desire by substituting something else for it. Or, surrender yourself to that which you think is the master, the saviour, the guru—which again is the activity of thought. This has been the pattern of all religious thinking. One has to understand the whole movement of desire; for obviously it is not love, nor yet compassion. Without love and compassion, meditation is utterly meaningless. Love and compassion have their own intelligence which is not the intelligence of cunning thought.

So it is important to understand the nature of desire, why it has played such an extraordinarily important part in our life; how it distorts clarity, how it prevents the extraordinary quality of love. It is important that we understand and do not suppress, do not try to control it or direct it in a particular direction, which you think may give you peace.

Please bear in mind that the speaker is not trying to impress you or guide and help you. But together we are walking a very subtle, complex path. We have to listen to each other to find out the truth about desire. When one understands the significance, the meaning, the fullness, the truth of desire, then desire has quite a different value or drive in one's life.

When one observes desire, is one observing it as an outsider looking at desire? Or is one observing desire as it arises? Not desire as something separate from oneself, one is desire. You see the difference? Either one observes desire, which one has when one sees something in the shop window which pleases one, and one has the desire to buy it so that the object is different from 'me', or else the desire is 'me', so there is a perception of desire without the observer watching desire.

One can look at a tree. *Tree* is the word by which one recognizes that which is standing in the field. But one knows that the word *tree* is not the tree. Similarly one's wife is not the word. But one has made the word one's wife. I do not know if you see all the subtleties of this. One must very clearly understand, from the beginning, that the word is not the thing. The word *desire* is not the feeling of it—the extraordinary feeling there is behind that reaction. So one must be very watchful that one is not caught in the word. Also the brain must be active enough to see that the object may create desire—desire which is separate from the object. Is one aware that the word is not the thing and that desire is not separate from the observer who is watching desire? Is one aware that the object may create desire but the desire is independent of the object?

How does desire flower? Why is there such extraordinary energy behind it? If we do not understand deeply the nature of desire we will always be in conflict with each other. One may desire one thing and one's wife may desire another and the children may desire something different. So we are always at loggerheads with each other. And this battle, this struggle, is called love, relationship.

We are asking: What is the source of desire? We must be very truthful in this, very honest, for desire is very very deceptive, very subtle, unless we understand the root of it. For all of us sensory responses are important—sight, touch, taste, smell, hearing. And a particular sensory response may for some of us be more important than the other responses. If we are artistic we see things in a special way. If we are trained as an engineer then the sensory responses are different. So we never observe totally, with all the sensory responses. We each respond somewhat specially, divided. Is it possible to respond totally with all one's senses? See the importance of that. If one responds totally with all one's senses there is the elimination of the centralized observer. But when one responds to a particular thing in a special way then the division begins. Find out when you leave this tent, when you look at the flowing waters of the river, the light sparkling on the swiftness of the waters, find out if you can look at it with all your senses. Do not ask me how, for that becomes mechanical. But educate yourself in the understanding of total sensory response.

When you see something, the seeing brings about a response. You see a green shirt, or a green dress, the seeing awakens the response. Then contact takes place. Then from contact thought creates the image of you in that shirt or dress, then the desire arises. Or you see a car in the road, it has nice lines, it is highly polished and there is plenty of power behind it. Then you go around it, examine the engine. Then thought creates the image of you getting into the car and starting the engine, putting your foot down and driving it. So does desire begin and the source of desire is thought creating the image, up to that point there is no desire. There are the sensory responses, which are normal, but then thought creates the image and from that moment desire begins. Now, is it possible for thought not to arise and create the image? This is learning about desire, which in itself is discipline. Learning about desire is discipline, not the controlling of it. If you really learn about something it is finished. But if you say you must control desire, then you are in a totally different field altogether. When you see the whole of this movement you will find that thought with its image will not interfere; you will only see, have the sensation. And what is wrong with that?

Saanen, Switzerland, July 19, 1981
The Network of Thought, pp. 44-8

It is not that you have no desire, but simply that the mind is capable of looking without describing.

Now, let us first see what happens to a mind that is always controlling itself, suppressing, sublimating desire. Such a mind, being occupied with itself, becomes insensitive. Though it may talk about sensitivity, goodness, though it may say that we must be brotherly, we must produce a marvellous world, and all the rest of the nonsense that people talk who suppress desire—such a mind is insensitive because it does not understand that which it has suppressed. Whether you suppress or yield to desire, it is essentially the same because the desire is still there. You may suppress the desire for a woman, for a car, for position; but the very urge not to have these things, which makes you suppress the desire for them, is itself a form of desire. So, being caught in desire, you have to understand it, and not say it is right or wrong.

Now, what is desire? When I see a tree swaying in the wind, it is a lovely thing to watch, and what is wrong with that? What is wrong in watching the beautiful motion of a bird on the wing? What is wrong in looking at a new car, marvellously built and highly polished? And what is wrong in seeing a nice person with a symmetrical face, a face that shows good sense, intelligence, quality?

But desire does not stop there. Your perception is not just perception, but with it comes sensation. With the arising of sensation you want to touch, to contact, and then comes the urge to possess. You say, "This is beautiful, I must have it," and so begins the turmoil of desire.

Now, is it possible to see, to observe, to be aware of the beautiful and the ugly things of life, and not say, "I must have," or "I must not have"? Have you ever just observed anything? Do you understand, sirs? Have you ever observed your wife, your children, your friends, just looked at them? Have you ever looked at a flower without calling it a rose, without wanting to put it in your buttonhole, or take it home and give it to somebody? If you are capable of so observing, without all the values attributed by the mind, then you will find that desire is not such a monstrous thing. You can look at a car, see the beauty of it, and not be caught in the turmoil or contradiction of desire. But that requires an immense intensity of observation, not just a casual glance. It is not that you have no desire, but simply that the mind is capable of looking without describing. It can look at the moon and not immediately say, "That is the moon, how beautiful it is," so there is no chattering of the mind coming in between. If you can do this, you will find that in the intensity of observation, of feeling, of real affection, love has its own action, which is not the contradictory action of desire.

Experiment with this and you will see how difficult it is for the mind to observe without chattering about what it observes. But surely, love is of that nature, is it not? How can you love if your mind is never silent, if you are always thinking about yourself? To love a person with your whole being, with your mind, heart, and body, requires great intensity; and when love is intense, desire soon disappears. But most of us have never had this intensity about anything, except about our own profit, conscious or unconscious; we never feel for anything without seeking something else out of it. But only the mind that has this intense energy is capable of following the swift movement of truth. Truth is not static, it is swifter than thought, and the mind cannot possibly conceive of it. To understand truth, there must be this immense energy which cannot be conserved or cultivated. This energy does not come through self-denial, through suppression. On the contrary, it demands complete abandonment, and you cannot abandon yourself, or abandon everything that you have, if you merely want a result.

It is possible to live without envy in this world which is based on envy, on acquisitiveness and the pursuit of power, position; but that requires an extraordinary intensity, a clarity of thought, of understanding. You cannot be free of envy without understanding yourself, so the beginning is here, not somewhere else. Unless you begin with yourself, do what you will, you will never find the end of sorrow.

Bombay, 2nd Public Talk, February 16, 1957
Collected Works, Vol. X, p. 245

You cannot become alive to desire if you condemn it or compare it.

So, the understanding of desire is necessary. You have "to understand desire," not "to be without desire." If you kill desire, you are paralysed. When you look at that sunset in front of you, the very looking is a delight, if you are at all sensitive. That is also desire—the delight. And if you cannot see that sunset and delight in it, you are not sensitive. If you cannot see a rich man in a big car and delight in that—not because you want it but you are just delighted to see a man in a big car—or if you cannot see a poor, unwashed, dirty, uneducated human being in despair and feel enormous pity, affection, love, you are not sensitive. How can you then find reality if you have not this sensitivity and feeling?

So you have to understand desire. And to understand every prompting of desire, you must have space, and not try to fill the space by your own thoughts or memories, or how to achieve, or how to destroy that desire. Then out of that understanding comes love. Most of us do not have love, we do not know what it means. We know pleasure, we know pain. We know the inconsistency of pleasure and, probably, the continuous pain. And we know the pleasure of sex and the pleasure of achieving fame, position, prestige, and the pleasure of having tremendous control over one's own body as the ascetics do, keeping a record—we know all these. We are everlastingly talking about love, but we do not know what it means, because we have not understood desire, which is the beginning of love.

Without love there is no morality—there is conformity to a pattern, a social or a so-called religious pattern. Without love there is no virtue. Love is something spontaneous, real, alive. And virtue is not a thing that you beget by constant practice; it is something spontaneous, akin to love. Virtue is not a memory according to which you function as a virtuous human being. If you have no love, you are not virtuous. You may go to the temple, you may lead a most respectable family life, you may have the social moralities, but you are not virtuous because your heart is barren, empty, dull, stupid, because you have not understood desire. Therefore life becomes an endless battleground, and effort ends always in death. Effort always ends in death, because that is all you know.

So, a man who would understand desire has to understand, has to listen, to every prompting of the mind and the heart, to every mood, to every change of thought and feeling, has to watch it; he has to become sensitive, become alive to it. You cannot become alive to desire if you condemn it or compare it. You must care for desire, because it will give you an enormous understanding. And out of that understanding there is sensitivity. You are then sensitive not only physically to beauty—to the dirt, to the stars, to a smiling face or to tears—but also to all the mutterings, the whispers that are in your minds, the secret hopes and fears.

And out of this listening, watching, comes passion, this passion which is akin to love. And it is only this state that can cooperate. And also it is only this state that can, because it can cooperate, know also when not to cooperate. Therefore, out of this depth of understanding, watching, the mind becomes efficient, clear, full of vitality, vigor; and it is only such a mind that can journey very far.

Madras, 4th Public Talk, January 22, 1964
Collected Works, Vol. XIV, pp. 99-100

Questioner: One seems to see the stupidity of desire and be free of it, but then it comes in again.

KRISHNAMURTI: I have never said that a free mind has no desire. After all, what is wrong with desire? The problem comes in when it creates conflict, when I want that lovely car which I cannot have. But to see the car—the beauty of its line, the color, the speed it can do—what is wrong with it? Is that desire to watch it, look at it, wrong? Desire only becomes urgent, compulsive when I want to possess that thing. We see that to be a slave to anything—to tobacco, to drink, to a particular way of thinking—implies desire, and that the effort to break away from the pattern also implies desire, and so we say we must come to a state where there is no desire. See how we shape life by our pettiness! And therefore our life becomes a mediocre affair, full of unknown fears and dark corners. But if we understand all that we have been talking about by seeing it actually, then I think desire has quite a different meaning.

Saanen, 4th Public Talk, August 1, 1961
Collected Works, Vol. XII, p. 201

The resistance to pain or the pursuit of pleasure—both give continuity to desire.

We are not saying that you must be without desire, or that you must suppress desire, as all your religious books say, or as all your gurus say. On the contrary, we are going to explore together into this question of desire. If you suppress desire, then you are destroying yourself, you are paralysing yourself, you are becoming insensitive, dull, stupid—as all religious people have done. To them, beauty, sensitivity, is denied, because they have suppressed. Whereas if you begin to understand the whole subtlety of desire, the nature of desire, then you will never suppress desire, you will never suppress anything—I will come to it later.

What is desire? Desire arises when you see a beautiful woman, a beautiful car, a well-dressed man, or a nice house. There is perception, sensation through contact, and then desire. I see you wearing a nice coat. There is perception, seeing; the attraction—the cut of that coat—and the sensation; and the desire to have that coat. This is very simple.

Now, what gives continuity to desire? You understand? I know how desire arises—that is fairly simple. What gives continuity to desire? It is this continuity of desire that strengthens, that becomes the will, obviously. Right? So I must find out what gives continuity to desire. If I can find out that, then I know how to deal with desire; I will never suppress it.

Now, what gives continuity to desire? I see something beautiful, attractive; a desire has been aroused. And I must find out now what gives it vitality, what gives it the continuity of its strength. There is something pleasurable which I feel desirable, and I give it continuity by thinking about it. One thinks about sex. You think about it and you give it a continuity. Or you think about the pain you had yesterday, the misery; and so you give that also continuity. So the arising of desire is natural, inevitable; you must have desire, you must react; otherwise you are a dead entity. But what is important is to see, to find out for yourself, when to give continuity to it and when not to.

So, you have to understand then the structure of thought, which influences and controls and shapes and gives continuity to desire. Right? That is clear. Thought functions according to memory and so on—into which we are not going now. We are just indicating how desire is strengthened by thinking about it constantly and giving it a continuity—which becomes the will. And with that will we operate. And that will is based on pleasure and on pain. If it is pleasurable, I want more of it; if it is painful, I resist it.

So, the resistance to pain or the pursuit of pleasure—both give continuity to desire. And when I understand this, there is never a question of suppression of desire, because when you suppress desire, it will inevitably bring about other conflicts—as in the case of suppressing a disease. You cannot suppress a disease; you have to bring it out; you have to go into it and do all kinds of things. But if you suppress it, it will gain in potency and become stronger and later will attack you. Similarly, when you understand the whole nature of desire and what gives continuity to desire, you will never, under any circumstances, suppress desire. But that does not mean that you indulge in desire. Because the moment you indulge in desire, it brings its own pain, its own pleasure, and you are back again in the vicious circle.

Bombay, 2nd Public Talk, February 14, 1965
Collected Works, Vol. XV, pp. 59-60

Desire would become a thing of flame . . .

We see how desire arises, which is quite simple. And then we have to find out what gives continuity to desire. That is the really important question—not how desire arises. We know how desire arises. I see something beautiful, I want it. I see something ugly, painful; that reminds me of all kinds of things: I put it away. One becomes aware of the arising of desire, but one has never gone into—at least, most of us have not gone into—the question of what gives it continuity and what brings, in that continuity, contradiction. If there was no contradiction—which is the battle between the good and the bad, between the pain and the pleasure, between fulfillment and frustration—if there was not this contradiction in desire and continuity in desire, if there was an understanding of that, then desire would have quite a different meaning. Then desire would become a thing of flame, would have a quality of an urgency, a beauty, a tremendous response—not a thing to be frightened of, to be destroyed, to be suffocated, to be denied.

Madras, 3rd Public Talk, December 23, 1964
Collected Works, Vol. XV, p. 18

Questioner: All religions teach the need of curbing the senses. Are the senses a hindrance to the discovery of truth?

KRISHNAMURTI: Let us find out the truth of the matter and not rely on what the various teachers and books have said, or on what your local guru has implanted in your mind.

We know the extraordinary sensitivity of the senses—the sense of touch, of hearing, of seeing, tasting, and smelling. To see a flower completely, to be aware of its color, of its delicate perfume and beauty, you have to have senses. It is when you see a beautiful man or woman, or a fine car, that the trouble begins, for then desire comes in. Let us go slowly.

You see a beautiful car. There is perception or seeing, sensation, contact, and finally desire. That is how desire comes into being. Then desire says, "It would be marvellous to own that car, I must have it," so you spend your life and energy in getting money to buy the car. But religion says, "It is very bad, it is evil to be worldly. Your senses will lead you astray, so you must subjugate, control them. Don't look at a woman, or don't look at a man; discipline yourself, sublimate your desire." So, you begin to curb your senses, which is the cultivation of insensitivity. Or seeing around you the ugliness, the dirt, all the squalor and misery, you shut it out and say, "That is evil; I must find God, truth." On the one hand you are suppressing, making the senses insensitive, and on the other you are trying to become sensitive to God; so your whole being is becoming insensitive. Do you understand, sirs? If you suppress desire in any form your mind is obviously made insensitive, though you may be seeking God.

So the problem is to understand desire and not to be a slave to it, which means being totally sensitive with your body, with your mind and heart—sensitive to beauty and to ugliness, to the sky, to the flowers, to birds on the wing, to the sunset on the water, to the faces around you, to hypocrisy, and to the falseness of your own illusions. To be sensitive to all that is what matters, and not merely to cultivate sensitivity towards truth and beauty while denying everything else. The very denial of everything else brings about insensitivity.

If you consider it, you will see that to suppress the senses, to make them insensitive to that which is tempestuous, contradictory, conflicting, sorrowful—as all the swamis, yogis, and religions insist—is to deny the whole depth and beauty and glory of existence. To understand the truth, you must have complete sensitivity. Do you understand, sirs? Reality demands your whole being; you must come to it with your body, mind, and heart, as a total human being, not with a mind paralysed and made insensitive through discipline. Then you will find that you need not be frightened of the senses because you will know how to deal with them, and they will not lead you astray. You will understand the senses, love them, see their whole significance, and then you will no longer torture yourself with suppression, control. Don't you see that, sirs?

Love is not divine love or married love or brotherly love—you know all the labels. Love is just love, without giving it a meaning of your own. When you love a flower with your whole being, which is not just to say, "How beautiful," and walk by, or when you love a human being completely, with all your mind, heart, and body, then you will find there is no desire in it, and therefore no conflict, no contradiction. It is desire that creates contradiction, misery, the conflict between *what is* and *what should be,* the ideal. The man who has suppressed his senses and made himself insensitive does not know what love is; therefore, though he meditate for the next ten thousand years, he will not find God. It is only when your whole being is made sensitive to everything—to the depth of your feelings, to all the extraordinary intricacies of your mind—and not just to what you call God, that desire ceases to be contradictory. Then there is an altogether different process taking place, which is not the process of desire. Love is its own eternity, and it has its own action.

Bombay, 1st Public Talk, February 6, 1957
Collected Works, Vol. X, pp. 235-6

Leave desire alone, either to let fly or wither away . . . that is the very essence of a mind which is not in conflict.

So far, we have always done something about desire, given it the right channel, the right slant, the right aim, the right end. And if the mind—which is conditioned, which is always thinking in terms of achievement through training, through education, and so on—is no longer trying to shape desire as something apart from itself; if the mind is no longer interfering with desire, if I may use that word, then what is wrong with desire? Then, is it the thing we have always known as desire? Please, sirs, go along with it, come with me.

You see, we have always thought of desire in terms of fulfillment, achieving, gaining, getting rich, inwardly or outwardly, in terms of avoidance, in terms of 'the more'. And when you see all that, and put it away, then the feeling, which we have so far called desire, has a totally different meaning, has it not? Then you can see a beautiful car, a lovely house, a lovely dress without any reaction of wanting, identifying.

Questioner: It is the contradictions in desire that make it so impossible to deal with it.

KRISHNAMURTI: Why are there contradictions, sir? Do please follow it through. I want to be rich, powerful, important, and yet I see the futility of it because I see that the big people, with all their titles and so forth, are just nobodies. So there is a contradiction. Now, why? Why is there this pull in different directions; why is it not all in one direction? Do you follow what I mean? If I want to be a politician, why not be a politician, and get on with it? Why is there this withdrawal from it? Do please let us discuss it for a few minutes.

Questioner: We are afraid of what might happen if we give ourselves over entirely to one desire.

KRISHNAMURTI: Have you given yourself to anything once, totally, completely?

Questioner: Once or twice, for a few minutes.

KRISHNAMURTI: Been completely in it? Perhaps sexually, but apart from that do you know when you have given yourself to something, totally? I question it.

Questioner: Perhaps in listening to music.

KRISHNAMURTI: Look, sir. A toy absorbs a child. You give a child a toy, and he is completely happy; he is not restless, he is taken up with it, completely *there.* Is that giving yourself to something? The politicians, the religious people—they give themselves over to something. Why? Because it means power, position, prestige. The idea of being a somebody absorbs them like a toy. When you identify yourself with something, is that giving yourself over to something? There are people who identify themselves with their country, their queen, their king, and so on, which is another form of absorption. Is that giving oneself over to something?

Questioner: Is it possible ever actually to give oneself over to something in so far as there is always a schism between?

KRISHNAMURTI: That's it, sir. That is exactly right. You see, we cannot give ourselves over to something.

Questioner: Is it possible to give oneself over to someone?

KRISHNAMURTI: We try to; we try to identify ourselves with the husband, the wife, the child, the name—but you know better than I do what happens, so, why talk about it? You see we are deviating from the thing we are talking about.

Questioner: A desire is right and good when it does not damage anything else.

KRISHNAMURTI: Is there wrong desire and right desire? You see, you are going back to the beginning; we covered the whole field, surely. Do you see how we have translated it already—the desire that is good and bad, worthwhile and not worthwhile, noble and ignoble, harmful and beneficial? Look deep into it. You have divided it, have you not? That very division is the cause of conflict. Having introduced the conflict by the division, you have then introduced a further problem: how to get rid of the conflict?

You see, sirs, we have been talking for fifty minutes, this evening, to see if one can really see the significance of desire. And when one really sees the significance of desire, which includes both the good and the bad, when one sees the total meaning of this conflict, this division—not just verbally, but comprehends it fully, puts one's teeth into it—then there is only desire. But, you see, we insist on evaluating it as good and bad, beneficial and nonbeneficial. I thought at the beginning we could wipe away this division, but it is not so easy; it requires application, perception, insight.

Questioner: Is it possible to get rid of the object and stay with the essence of desire?

KRISHNAMURTI: Why should I get rid of the object? What is wrong with a beautiful car? You see, you are creating conflict for yourself when you make this division of the essence and the object. The direction of the essence changes the object all the time, and that is the misery of it. When one is young, one wants the world; and as one grows older, one is fed up with the world.

You see, we were trying to understand desire and thereby let conflict die away, wither away. We have touched on so many things this evening. The urge for power which is so strong in all of us, so embedded, and which includes the dominance over the servant, the husband, the wife—you know it all. Perhaps some of you, in the course of the discussion this evening, have gone into this thing, have seen that where the mind is seeking fulfillment, there is frustration and therefore misery and conflict. The very seeing of it is the dropping of it. Perhaps some of you have not merely followed the words but understood the implications of the feeling of wanting to fulfill, to be something—the ignobleness of it. The politician seeks fulfillment, the priest does it, everybody does it, and one sees the vulgarity of it all, if I may use that word. Can one really drop it? If you see it as you see a poisonous thing, then it is like a tremendous burden taken off your shoulders. You are out of it; with a flick, it is gone. Then you will come to that point which is really extraordinarily significant. Not all this—all this has its own significance—but something else, which is a mind that has understood desire, the feeling and the thought, and therefore goes beyond and above it. Do you understand the nature of such a mind—not the verbal description of it? The mind, then, is highly sensitive, capable of intense reactions without conflict, sensitive to every form of demand; such a mind is above all feeling and thought, and its activity is no longer within the field of so-called desire.

For most of us, I am afraid, this is a lot of froth, a state to be desired or created. But you cannot come to it that way nor by any means. It comes into being when one really understands all this, and you do not have to do a thing.

You see—if you will not misunderstand what is being said—if you could leave desire alone, either to let fly or wither away—just leave it alone—that is the very essence of a mind which is not in conflict.

London, 7th Public Talk, May 16, 1961
Collected Works, Vol. XII, pp. 150-3

We shall find that love and desire and passion are the same thing. If you destroy one, you destroy the other.

We have to understand desire, and it is very difficult to understand something which is so vital, so demanding, so urgent, because in the very fulfillment of desire, passion is engendered, with the pleasure and the pain of it. And if one is to understand desire, obviously, there must be no choice. You cannot judge desire as being good or bad, noble or ignoble, or say, "I will keep this desire and deny that one." All that must be set aside if we are to find out the truth of desire—the beauty of it, the ugliness, or whatever it may be. It is a very curious thing to consider, but here in the West, the Occident, many desires can be fulfilled. You have cars, prosperity, better health, the ability to read books, acquire knowledge, and accumulate various types of experience; whereas, when you go to the Orient, they are still wanting food, clothing, and shelter, still caught in the misery and degradation of poverty. But in the West as well as in the East desire is burning all the time, in every direction; outward and deep within, it is there. The man who renounces the world is as crippled by his desire to pursue God as the man who pursues prosperity. So it is there all the time, burning, contradicting itself, creating turmoil, anxiety, guilt, and despair.

I do not know if you have ever experimented with it at all. But what happens if you do not condemn desire, do not judge it as being good or bad, but simply be aware of it? I wonder if you know what it means to be aware of something? Most of us are not aware because we have become so accustomed to condemning, judging, evaluating, identifying, choosing. Choice obviously prevents awareness because choice is always made as a result of conflict. To be aware when you enter a room, to see all the furniture, the carpet or its absence, and so on—just to see it, to be aware of it all without any sense of judgment—is very difficult. Have you ever tried to look at a person, a flower, at an idea, an emotion, without any choice, any judgment?

And if one does the same thing with desire, if one lives with it—not denying it or saying, "What shall I do with this desire? It is so ugly, so rampant, so violent," not giving it a name, a symbol, not covering it with a word—then, is it any longer the cause of turmoil? Is desire then something to be put away, destroyed? We want to destroy it because one desire tears against another, creating conflict, misery, and contradiction; and one can see how one tries to escape from this everlasting conflict. So can one be aware of the totality of desire? What I mean by totality is not just one desire or many desires, but the total quality of desire itself. And one can be aware of the totality of desire only when there is no opinion about it, no word, no judgment, no choice. To be aware of every desire as it arises, not to identify oneself with it or condemn it, in that state of alertness, is it then desire, or is it a flame, a passion that is necessary? The word *passion* is generally kept for one thing—sex. But for me, passion is not sex. You must have passion, intensity, to really live with anything; to live fully, to look at a mountain, a tree, to really look at a human being, you must have passionate intensity. But that passion, that flame is denied when you are hedged around by various urges, demands, contradictions, fears. How can a flame survive when it is smothered by a lot of smoke? Our life is but smoke; we are looking for the flame but we are denying it by suppressing, controlling, shaping the thing we call desire.

Without passion how can there be beauty? I do not mean the beauty of pictures, buildings, painted women, and all the rest of it. They have their own forms of beauty, but we are not talking of superficial beauty. A thing put together by man, like a cathedral, a temple, a picture, a poem, or a statue may or may not be beautiful. But there is a beauty which is beyond feeling and thought and which cannot be realized, understood, or known if there is not passion. So do not misunderstand the word *passion*. It is not an ugly word; it is not a thing you can buy in the market or talk about romantically. It has nothing whatever to do with emotion, feeling. It is not a respectable thing; it is a flame that destroys anything that is false. And we are always so afraid to allow that flame to devour the things that we hold dear, the things that we call important.

After all, the lives we lead at present, based on needs, desires, and the ways of controlling desire, make us more shallow and empty than ever. We may be very clever, very learned, able to repeat what we have gathered, but the electronic machines are doing that, and already in some fields the machines are more capable than man, more accurate and swifter in their calculations. So we always come back to the same thing—which is that life as we live it now is so very superficial, narrow, limited, all because deep down we are empty, lonely, and always trying to cover it up, to fill up that emptiness; therefore, the need, the desire becomes a terrible thing. Nothing can fill that deep void within—no gods, no saviors, no knowledge, no relationship, no children, no husband, no wife—nothing. But if the mind, the brain, the whole of your being can look at it, live with it, then you will see that psychologically, inwardly, there is no need for anything. That is true freedom.

But that requires very deep insight, profound inquiry, ceaseless watching; and out of that perhaps we shall know what love is. How can there be love when there is attachment, jealousy, envy, ambition, and all the pretence which goes with that word? Then, if we have gone through that emptiness—which is an actuality, not a myth, not an idea—we shall find that love and desire and passion are the same thing. If you destroy one, you destroy the other; if you corrupt one, you corrupt beauty. To go into all this requires, not a detached mind, not a dedicated mind or a religious mind, but a mind that is inquiring, that is never satisfied, that is always looking, watching, observing itself, knowing itself. Without love you will never find out what truth is.

Paris, 4th Public Talk, September 12, 1961
Collected Works, Vol. XII, pp. 244-6

IV. Why Has Sex Become a Problem?

When there is no love in your heart, you have only one thing left, which is pleasure; and that pleasure is sex, and therefore it becomes a mountainous problem. To resolve it, you have to understand it. When you understand it, you begin to free the mind.

New Delhi, 4th Public Talk, December 25, 1966
Collected Works, Vol. XVII, p. 130

Many things are involved in sex, not just the act.

What is sex? Is it the act, or the pleasurable images, the thought, the memories around it all? Or, is it just a biological fact? And is there the memory, the picture, the excitement, the need when there is love—if I may use that word without spoiling it? I think one has to understand the physical, biological fact. That is one thing. All the romanticism, the excitement, the feeling that one has given oneself over to another, the identification of oneself with another in that relationship, the sense of continuity, the satisfaction—all that is another thing. When we are really concerned with desire, with need, how deeply does sex play a part? Is it a psychological need, as it is a biological need? It requires a very clear, sharp mind, brain, to differentiate between the physical need and the psychological need. Many things are involved in sex, not just the act. The desire to forget oneself in another, the continuity of a relationship, children, and trying to find immortality through the children, the wife, the husband, the sense of giving oneself over to another, with all the problems of jealousy, attachment, fear—the agony of it all—is all that love? If there is no understanding of need, basically, deep down, completely, in the dark recesses of one's own consciousness, then sex, love, and desire play havoc in our lives.

Paris, 4th Public Talk, September 12, 1961
Collected Works, Vol. XII, p. 247

Questioner: We know sex as an inescapable physical and psychological necessity and it seems to be a root cause of chaos in the personal life of our generation. How can we deal with this problem?

KRISHNAMURTI: Why is it that whatever we touch we turn into a problem? We have made God a problem, we have made love a problem, we have made relationship, living a problem, and we have made sex a problem. Why? Why is everything we do a problem, a horror? Why are we suffering? Why has sex become a problem? Why do we submit to living with problems, why do we not put an end to them? Why do we not die to our problems instead of carrying them day after day, year after year? Sex is certainly a relevant question but there is the primary question, why do we make life into a problem? Working, sex, earning money, thinking, feeling, experiencing—you know, the whole business of living—why is it a problem? Is it not essentially because we always think from a particular point of view, from a fixed point of view? We are always thinking from a center towards the periphery but the periphery is the center for most of us and so anything we touch is superficial. But life is not superficial; it demands living completely, and because we are living only superficially we know only superficial reaction. Whatever we do on the periphery must inevitably create a problem, and that is our life: we live in the superficial and we are content to live there with all the problems of the superficial. Problems exist so long as we live in the superficial, on the periphery, the periphery being the 'me' and its sensations, which can be externalized or made subjective, which can be identified with the universe, with the country, or with some other thing made up by the mind.

So long as we live within the field of the mind there must be complications, there must be problems; that is all we know. Mind is sensation, mind is the result of accumulated sensations and reactions, and anything it touches is bound to create misery, confusion, an endless problem. The mind is the real cause of our problems, the mind that is working mechanically night and day, consciously and unconsciously. The mind is a most superficial thing and we have spent generations, we spend our whole lives, cultivating the mind, making it more and more clever, more and more subtle, more and more cunning, more and more dishonest and crooked, all of which is apparent in every activity of our life. The very nature of our mind is to be dishonest, crooked, incapable of facing facts, and that is the thing which creates problems; that is the thing which is the problem itself.

What do we mean by the problem of sex? Is it the act, or is it a thought about the act? Surely it is not the act. The sexual act is no problem to you, any more than eating is a problem to you, but if you *think* about eating or anything else all day long because you have nothing else to think about, it becomes a problem to you. Is the sexual act the problem or is it the thought about the act? Why do you think about it? Why do you build it up, which you are obviously doing? The cinemas, the magazines, the stories, the way women dress, everything is building up your thought of sex. Why does the mind build it up, why does the mind think about sex at all? Why? Why has it become a central issue in your life? When there are so many things calling, demanding your attention, you give complete attention to the thought of sex. What happens, why are your minds so occupied with it? Because that is a way of ultimate escape, is it not? It is a way of complete self-forgetfulness. For the time being, at least for that moment, you can forget yourself—and there is no other way of forgetting yourself. Everything else you do in life gives emphasis to the 'me', to the self. Your business, your religion, your gods, your leaders, your political and economic actions, your escapes, your social activities, your joining one party and rejecting another—all that is emphasizing and giving strength to the 'me'. That is, there is only one act in which there is no emphasis on the 'me', so it becomes a problem, does it not? When there is only one thing in your life which is an avenue to ultimate escape to complete forgetfulness of yourself if only for a few seconds, you cling to it because that is the only moment in which you are happy. Every other issue you touch becomes a nightmare, a source of suffering and pain, so you cling to the one thing which gives complete self-forgetfulness, which you call happiness. But when you cling to it, it too becomes a nightmare, because then you want to be free from it, you do not want to be a slave to it. So you invent, again from the mind, the idea of chastity, of celibacy, and you try to be celibate, to be chaste, through suppression, all of which are operations of the mind to cut itself off from the fact. This again gives particular emphasis to the 'me' who is trying to become something, so again you are caught in travail, in trouble, in effort, in pain.

Sex becomes an extraordinarily difficult and complex problem so long as you do not understand the mind which thinks about the problem. The act itself can never be a problem, but the thought about the act creates the problem. The act you safeguard; you live loosely, or indulge yourself in marriage, thereby making your wife into a prostitute, which is all apparently very respectable, and you are satisfied to leave it at that. Surely the problem can be solved only when you understand the whole process and structure of the 'me' and the 'mine': my wife, my child, my property, my car, my achievement, my success; until you understand and resolve all that, sex as a problem will remain. So long as you are ambitious, politically, religiously or in any way, so long as you are emphasizing the self, the thinker, the experiencer, by feeding him on ambition—whether in the name of yourself as an individual or in the name of the country, of the party, or of an idea which you call religion—so long as there is this activity of self-expansion, you will have a sexual problem.

You are creating, feeding, expanding yourself on the one hand, and on the other you are trying to forget yourself, to lose yourself if only for a moment. How can the two exist together? Your life is a contradiction; emphasis on the 'me' and forgetting the 'me'. Sex is not a problem; the problem is this contradiction in your life; and the contradiction cannot be bridged over by the mind, because the mind itself is a contradiction. The contradiction can be understood only when you understand fully the whole process of your daily existence. Going to the cinemas and watching women on the screen, reading books which stimulate the thought, the magazines with their half-naked pictures, your way of looking at women, the surreptitious eyes that catch yours—all these things are encouraging the mind through devious ways to emphasize the self and at the same time you try to be kind, loving, tender. The two cannot go together. The man who is ambitious, spiritually or otherwise, can never be without a problem, because problems cease only when the self is forgotten, when the 'me' is non-existent, and that state of the non-existence of the self is not an act of will, it is not a mere reaction. Sex becomes a reaction; when the mind tries to solve the problem, it only makes the problem more confused, more troublesome, more painful. The act is not the problem, but the mind is the problem, the mind which says it must be chaste. Chastity is not of the mind. The mind can only suppress its own activities and suppression is not chastity. Chastity is not a virtue, chastity cannot be cultivated. The man who is cultivating humility is surely not a humble man; he may call his pride humility, but he is a proud man, and that is why he seeks to become humble. Pride can never become humble, and chastity is not a thing of the mind—you cannot become chaste. You will know chastity only when there is love, and love is not of the mind nor a thing of the mind.

Therefore, the problem of sex, which tortures so many people all over the world, cannot be resolved till the mind is understood. We cannot put an end to thinking but thought comes to an end when the thinker ceases, and the thinker ceases only when there is an understanding of the whole process. Fear comes into being when there is division between the thinker and his thought; when there is no thinker, then only is there no conflict in thought. What is implicit needs no effort to understand. The thinker comes into being through thought; then the thinker exerts himself to shape, to control his thoughts or to put an end to them. The thinker is a fictitious entity, an illusion of the mind. When there is a realization of thought as a fact, then there is no need to think about the fact. If there is simple, choiceless awareness, then that which is implicit in the fact begins to reveal itself; therefore, thought as fact ends. Then you will see that the problems which are eating at our hearts and minds, the problems of our social structure, can be resolved. Then sex is no longer a problem, it has its proper place, it is neither an impure thing nor a pure thing. Sex has its place; but when the mind gives it the predominant place, then it becomes a problem. The mind gives sex a predominant place because it cannot live without some happiness, and so sex becomes a problem; when the mind understands its whole process and so comes to an end, that is when thinking ceases, then there is creation and it is that creation which makes us happy. To be in that state of creation is bliss, because it is self-forgetfulness in which there is no reaction as from the self. This is not an abstract answer to the daily problem of sex—it is the only answer. The mind denies love and without love there is no chastity; it is because there is no love that you make sex into a problem.

The First and Last Freedom, pp. 227-31

What most people are concerned with is the passion of lust.

KRISHNAMURTI: Thought, in its very nature, is divisive. It is thought that seeks pleasure and holds it. It is thought that cultivates desire.

Questioner: Will you go into desire a bit more?

KRISHNAMURTI: There is the seeing of a house, the sensation that it is lovely, then there is the desire to own it and to have pleasure from it, then there is the effort to get it. All this constitutes the center, and this center is the cause of division. This center is the feeling of a 'me', which is the cause of division, because this very feeling of 'me' is the feeling of separation. People have called this the ego and all kinds of other names—the 'lower self' as opposed to some idea of a 'higher self'—but there is no need to be complicated about it; it is very simple. Where there is the center, which is the feeling of 'me', which in its activities isolates itself, there is division and resistance. And all this is the process of thought. So when you ask what is love, it is not of this center. Love is not pleasure and pain, nor hate, nor violence in any form.

Questioner: Therefore, in this love you speak of there can be no sex, because there cannot be desire?

KRISHNAMURTI: Don't, please, come to any conclusion. We are investigating, exploring. Any conclusion or assumption prevents further enquiry. To answer this question we have also to look at the energy of thought. Thought, as we have said, sustains pleasure by thinking about something that has been pleasurable, cultivating the image, the picture. Thought engenders pleasure. Thinking about the sexual act becomes lust, which is entirely different from the act of sex. What most people are concerned with is the passion of lust. Craving before and after sex is lust. This craving is thought. Thought is not love.

Questioner: Can there be sex without this desire of thought?

KRISHNAMURTI: You have to find out for yourself. Sex plays an extraordinarily important part in our lives because it is perhaps the only deep, first-hand experience we have. Intellectually and emotionally we conform, imitate, follow, obey. There is pain and strife in all our relationships, except in the act of sex. This act, being so different and beautiful, we become addicted to, so it in turn becomes a bondage. The bondage is the demand for its continuation—again the action of the center which is divisive. One is so hedged about—intellectually, in the family, in the community, through social morality, through religious sanctions—so hedged about that there is only this one relationship left in which there is freedom and intensity; therefore, we give tremendous importance to it. But if there were freedom all around then this would not be such a craving and such a problem. We make it a problem because we can't get enough of it, or because we feel guilty at having got it, or because in getting it we break the rules which society has laid down. It is the old society which calls the new society permissive because for the new society sex is a part of life. In freeing the mind from the bondage of imitation, authority, conformity, and religious prescriptions, sex has its own place, but it won't be all-consuming. From this, one can see that freedom is essential for love—not the freedom of revolt, not the freedom of doing what one likes, nor of indulging openly or secretly one's cravings, but rather the freedom which comes in the understanding of this whole structure and nature of the center. Then, freedom is love.

Questioner: So freedom is not license?

KRISHNAMURTI: No. License is bondage. Love is not hate, nor jealousy, nor ambition, nor the competitive spirit with its fear of failure. It is not the love of God nor the love of man—which again is a division. Love is not of the one or of the many. When there is love, it is personal and impersonal, with and without an object. It is like the perfume of a flower; one or many can smell it: what matters is the perfume, not to whom it belongs.

Second Penguin Krishnamurti Reader, pp. 238-40

When there is love, sex is never a problem.

When we are young, we have strong sexual urges, and most of us try to deal with these desires by controlling and disciplining them, because we think that without some kind of restraint we shall become consumingly lustful. Organized religions are much concerned about our sexual morality; but they allow us to perpetrate violence and murder in the name of patriotism, to indulge in envy and crafty ruthlessness, and to pursue power and success. Why should they be so concerned with this particular type of morality, and not attack exploitation, greed, and war? Is it not because organized religions, being part of the environment which we have created, depend for their very existence on our fears and hopes, on our envy and separatism? So, in the religious field as in every other, the mind is held in the projections of its own desires.

As long as there is no deep understanding of the whole process of desire, the institution of marriage as it now exists, whether in the East or in the West, cannot provide the answer to the sexual problem. Love is not induced by the signing of a contract, nor is it based on an exchange of gratification, nor on mutual security and comfort. All these things are of the mind, and that is why love occupies so small a place in our lives. Love is not of the mind; it is wholly independent of thought with its cunning calculations, its self-protective demands and reactions. When there is love, sex is never a problem—it is the lack of love that creates the problem.

The hindrances and escapes of the mind constitute the problem, and not sex or any other specific issue; and that is why it is important to understand the mind's process, its attractions and repulsions, its responses to beauty, to ugliness.

Education and the Significance of Life, pp. 117-18

A man who loves is pure, though he may be sexual.

It is the man who is intellectual, full of knowledge—knowledge being different from wisdom—the man who has schemes, who wants to save the world, who is full of intellection, full of mentation: it is he who is caught up in sex. Because his life is shallow, his heart empty, sex becomes important—and that is what is happening in the present civilization. We have overcultivated our intellect, and the mind is caught in its own creations as the radio, the motorcar, the mechanized amusements, the technical knowledge, and the various addictions the mind indulges in. When such a mind is caught, there is only one release for it, which is sex. Sirs, look at what is happening within each one of us, don't look at somebody else. Examine your own life and you will see how you are caught in this problem, how extraordinarily empty your life is. What is your life, sirs? Bright, arid, empty, dull, weary, is it not? You go to your offices, do your jobs, repeat your mantras, perform your pujas. When you are in the office, you are subjugated, dull, you have to follow a routine; you have become mechanical in your religion; it is mere acceptance of authority. So, religiously, in the world of business, in your education, in your daily life, what is actually happening? There is no creative state of being, is there? You are not happy, you are not vital, you are not joyous. Intellectually, religiously, economically, socially, politically, you are dull, regimented, are you not? This regimentation is the result of your own fears, your own hopes, your own frustrations; and since for a human being so caught there is no release, naturally he looks to sex for a release—there he can indulge himself, there he can seek happiness. So, sex becomes automatic, habitual, routine, and that also becomes a dulling, a vicious process. That is your life, actually, if you look at it, if you don't try to dodge it, if you don't try to excuse it. The actual fact is, you are not creative. You may have babies, innumerable babies, but that is not creative action, that is an accidental action of existence.

So, a mind that is not alert, vital, a heart that is not affectionate, full, how can it be creative? And not being creative, you seek stimulation through sex, through amusement, cinemas, theaters, through watching others play while you remain a spectator; others paint the scene or dance, and you yourself are but an observer. That is not creation. Similarly, so many books are printed in the world because you merely read. You are not the creator. Where there is no creation, the only release is through sex, and then you make your wife or husband the prostitute. Sirs, you have no idea of the implications, the wickedness, the cruelty of all this. I know you are uncomfortable. You are not thinking it out. You are shutting your mind, and therefore sex has become an immense problem in modern civilization—either promiscuity, or the mechanical habit of sexual release in marriage. Sex will remain a problem as long as there is no creative state of being. You may use birth control, you may adopt various practices, but you are not free of sex. Sublimation is not freedom, suppression is not freedom, control is not freedom. There is freedom only when there is affection, when there is love. Love is pure, and when that is missing, your trying to become pure through the sublimation of sex is mere stupidity. The factor that purifies is love, not your desire to be pure. A man who loves is pure, though he may be sexual; and without love, sex is what it is now in your lives—a routine, an ugly process, a thing to be avoided, ignored, done away with, or indulged in.

Bangalore, 6th Public Talk, August 8, 1948
Collected Works, Vol. V, pp. 55-6

If you deny sexuality, you must close your eyes . . . and never look at anything.

KRISHNAMURTI: What do you mean by sexual feeling? To look at a woman? All the biological urges? And to look at a tree, is that not also sexuality? To look at a flower which has great beauty, that's a form of sensuality too, isn't it? No?

Questioner: Yes.

KRISHNAMURTI: So if you deny—as most religions have denied—sexuality, then you must close your eyes, cut your tongue, put out your eyes, and never look at anything. Don't laugh, sirs, this is what you're doing anyhow, because you are not aware of beauty at all. To you, beauty is associated with a woman or with a man. Therefore, the Shankaras of the world have said, "Don't have anything to do with woman, if you want to be spiritual." So you deny the whole beauty of the earth.

Have you ever stopped and looked at a tree, looked at a flower? Have you ever looked at a woman or a man who is beautiful, and not said, "I want to get something out of her"—just looked at the beauty of something, of the hills, the trees, the flowers, the faces, the smiles? You haven't, and therefore you don't know what love is or beauty is. All that you know is "you must not" and "you must." So, you have starved your heart and your mind—you are dehydrated human beings. And you smile and accept it and carry on.

So, sirs, the first thing is not to condemn, and then you will know what love is.

Rishi Valley, India, November 9, 1967

If [sexual feeling] is born out of love it is not lust, even though great delight may then be present.

Questioner: What is passion?

KRISHNAMURTI: I think we should be clear that lust and passion are two different things. Lust is sustained by thought, driven by thought, it grows and gathers substance in thought until it explodes sexually, or, if it is the lust for power, in its own violent forms of fulfillment. Passion is something entirely different; it is not the product of thought, nor the remembrance of a past event; it is not driven by any motive of fulfillment; it is not sorrow, either.

Questioner: Is all sexual passion lust? Sexual response is not always the result of thought; it may be contact as when you suddenly meet somebody whose loveliness overpowers you.

KRISHNAMURTI: Wherever thought builds up the image of pleasure it must inevitably be lust, and not the freedom of passion. If pleasure is the main drive, then it is lust. When sexual feeling is born out of pleasure it is lust. If it is born out of love it is not lust, even though great delight may then be present. Here we must be clear and find out for ourselves whether love excludes pleasure and enjoyment. When you see a cloud and delight in its vastness and the light on it, there is of course pleasure, but there is a great deal more than pleasure. We are not condemning this at all. If you keep returning to the cloud in thought, or in fact, for a stimulation, then you are indulging in an imaginative flight of fancy, and obviously here pleasure and thought are the incentives operating. When you first looked at that cloud and saw its beauty there was no such incentive of pleasure operating. The beauty in sex is the absence of the 'me', the ego, but the thought of sex is the affirmation of this ego, and that is pleasure. This ego is all the time either seeking pleasure or avoiding pain, wanting fulfillment and thereby inviting frustration. In all this the feeling of passion is sustained and pursued by thought, and therefore it is no longer passion but pleasure. The hope, the pursuit, of remembered passion is pleasure.

Questioner: What is passion itself, then?

KRISHNAMURTI: It has to do with joy and ecstasy, which is not pleasure. In pleasure there is always a subtle form of effort—a seeing, striving, demanding, struggling to keep it, to get it. In passion there is no demand and therefore no struggle. In passion there is not the slightest shadow of fulfillment, therefore there can be neither frustration nor pain. Passion is the freedom from the 'me', which is the center of all fulfillment and pain. Passion does not demand because it *is,* and I am not speaking of something static. Passion is the austerity of self-abnegation in which the 'you' and the 'me' is not; therefore passion is the essence of life. It is this that moves and lives. But when thought brings in all the problems of having and holding, then passion ceases. Without passion, creation is not possible.

Questioner: What do you mean by creation?

KRISHNAMURTI: Freedom.

Questioner: What freedom?

KRISHNAMURTI: Freedom from the 'me' which depends on environment and is the product of environment—the me which is put together by society and thought. This freedom is clarity, the light that is not lit from the past. Passion is only the present.

Questioner: This has fired me with a strange new feeling.

KRISHNAMURTI: That is the passion of learning.

Questioner: What particular action in my daily living will ensure that this passion is burning and operating?

KRISHNAMURTI: Nothing will ensure it except the attention of learning, which is action, which is now. In this there is the beauty of passion, which is the total abandonment of the 'me' and its time.

Second Penguin Krishnamurti Reader, pp. 296-8

When there is love, the sexual act has quite a different significance.

How is it possible to meet the sexual demand intelligently and not turn it into a problem?

Now, what do we mean by sex? The purely physical act, or the thought that excites, stimulates, furthers that act? Surely, sex is of the mind, and because it is of the mind, it must seek fulfillment, or there is frustration. Do not be nervous about the subject. You have all become very tense, I see. Let us talk it over as though it were any other subject. Don't look so grave and lost! Let us deal with this subject very simply and directly. The more complex a subject is, the more it demands clear thinking, the more must it be approached simply and directly.

Why is it that sex has become such a problem in our lives? Let us go into it, not with constraint, not with anxiety, fear, condemnation. Why has it become a problem? Surely, for most of you it is a problem. Why? Probably, you have never asked yourself why it is a problem. Let us find out.

Sex is a problem because it would seem that in that act there is complete absence of the self. In that moment you are happy, because there is the cessation of self-consciousness, of the 'me'; and desiring more of it—more of the abnegation of the self in which there is complete happiness, without the past or the future, demanding that complete happiness through full fusion, integration—naturally it becomes all-important. Isn't that so? Because it is something that gives me unadulterated joy, complete self forgetfulness, I want more and more of it. Now, why do I want more of it? Because, everywhere else I am in conflict, everywhere else, at all the different levels of existence, there is the strengthening of the self. Economically, socially, religiously, there is the constant thickening of self-consciousness, which is conflict. After all, you are self-conscious only when there is conflict. Self-consciousness is in its very nature the result of conflict. So, everywhere else we are in conflict. In all our relationships with property, with people, with ideas there is conflict, pain, struggle, misery; but in this one act there is complete cessation of all that. Naturally you want more of it because it gives you happiness, while all the rest leads you to misery, turmoil, conflict, confusion, antagonism, worry, destruction; therefore, the sexual act becomes all-significant, all-important.

So, the problem is not sex, surely, but how to be free from the self. You have tasted that state of being in which the self is not, if only for a few seconds, if only for a day, or what you will; and where the self is, there is conflict, there is misery, there is strife. So, there is the constant longing for more of that self-free state. But the central problem is the conflict at different levels and how to abnegate the self. You are seeking happiness—that state in which the self, with all its conflicts, is not—which you find momentarily in that act. Or, you discipline yourself, you struggle, you control, you even destroy yourself through suppression—which means you are seeking to be free of conflict because with the cessation of conflict there is joy. If there can be freedom from conflict, then there is happiness at all the different levels of existence.

What makes for conflict? How does this conflict arise in your work, in your relationships, in teaching, in everything? Even when you write a poem, even when you sing, when you paint, there is conflict.

How does this conflict come into being? Does it not come into being through the desire to become? You paint, you want to express yourself through color, you want to be the best painter. You study, worry, hope that the world will acclaim your painting. But, wherever there is the desire to become the 'more', there must be conflict. It is the psychological urge that demands the 'more'. The need for more is psychological, the urge for the 'more' exists when the psyche, the mind is becoming, seeking, pursuing an end, a result. When you want to be a mahatma, when you want to be a saint, when you want to understand, when you are practicing virtue, when you are class-conscious as a "superior" entity, when you subserve function to heighten yourself—all these are indications, obviously, of a mind that is becoming. The 'more', therefore, is conflict. A mind which is seeking the 'more' is never conscious of *what is,* because it is always living in the 'more'—in what it would like to be, never in *what is.* Until you resolve the whole content of that conflict, this one release of the self, through sex, will remain a hideous problem.

Sirs, the self is not an objective entity that can be studied under the microscope or learned through books or understood through quotations, however weighty those quotations may be. It can be understood only in relationship. After all, conflict is in relationship, whether with property, with an idea, with your wife, or with your neighbor; and without solving that fundamental conflict, merely to hold onto that one release through sex, is obviously to be unbalanced. And that is exactly what we are. We are unbalanced because we have made sex the one avenue of escape; and society, so-called modern culture, helps us to do it. Look at the advertisements, the cinemas, the suggestive gestures, postures, appearances.

Most of you married when you were quite young, when the biological urge was very strong. You took a wife or a husband, and with that wife or husband you jolly well have to live for the rest of your life. Your relationship is merely physical, and everything else has to be adjusted to that. So what happens? You are intellectual, perhaps, and she is very emotional. Where is your communion with her? Or she is very practical, and you are dreamy, vague, rather indifferent. Where is the contact between you and her? You are oversexed, and she is not; but you use her because you have rights. How can there be communion between you and her when you use her? Our marriages are now based on that idea, on that urge; but more and more there are contradictions and great conflicts in marriage, and so divorces.

So, this problem requires intelligent handling, which means that we have to alter the whole basis of our education; and that demands understanding not only the facts of life but also our every day existence, not only knowing and understanding the biological urge, the sexual urge, but also seeing how to deal with it intelligently. But now we don't do that, do we? It is a hushed subject, it is a secret thing, only talked about behind walls. When the urge is very strong, irrespective of anything else, we get mated for the rest of our life. See what one has done to oneself and to another.

How can the intellectual meet, commune, with the sentimental, the dull, or with the one who is not educated? And what communion is there then, except the sexual? The difficulty in all this is, is it not, that the fulfillment of the sexual urge, the biological urge, necessitates certain social regulations; therefore, you have marriage laws. You have all the ways of possessing that which gives you pleasure, security, comfort; but that which gives constant pleasure dulls the mind. As constant pain dulls the mind, so constant pleasure withers the mind and heart.

And how can you have love? Surely, love is not a thing of the mind, is it? Love is not merely the sexual act, is it? Love is something which the mind cannot possibly conceive; love is something which cannot be formulated. And, without love, you become related; without love, you marry. Then, in that marriage, you "adjust yourselves" to each other. Lovely phrase! You adjust yourselves to each other, which is again an intellectual process, is it not? She has married you, but you are an ugly lump of flesh, carried away by your passions. She has got to live with you. She does not like the house, the surroundings, the hideousness of it, your brutality. But she says, "Yes, I am married, I have got to put up with it." So, as a means of self-protection, she yields, she presently begins to say, "I love you." You know, when, through the desire for security, we put up with something ugly, that ugly thing seems to become beautiful because it is a form of self-protection; otherwise, we might be hurt, we might be utterly destroyed. So we see that which was ugly, hideous, has become gradually beautiful.

This adjustment is obviously a mental process—all adjustments are. But, surely, love is incapable of adjustment. You know, sirs, don't you, that if you love another, there is no "adjustment": there is only complete fusion. Only when there is no love do we begin to adjust. And this adjustment is called marriage. Hence, marriage fails because it is the very source of conflict, a battle between two people. It is an extraordinarily complex problem, like all problems, but more so because the appetites, the urges, are so strong.

So, a mind which is merely adjusting itself can never be chaste. A mind which is seeking happiness through sex can never be chaste. Though you may momentarily have, in that act, self-abnegation, self-forgetfulness, the very pursuit of that happiness, which is of the mind, makes the mind unchaste. Chastity comes into being only where there is love. Without love, there is no chastity. And love is not a thing to be cultivated. There is love only when there is complete self-forgetfulness, and to have the blessing of that love, one must be free through understanding relationship. Then, when there is love, the sexual act has quite a different significance; then that act is not an escape, is not habit. Love is not an ideal; love is a state of being. Love cannot be where there is becoming. Only where love is, is there chastity, purity; but a mind that is becoming, or attempting to become chaste, has no love.

Banaras, 5th Public Talk, February 20, 1949
Collected Works, Vol. V, pp. 216-18

V. On Chastity

The person who has taken the vow of celibacy knows no love, because he is concerned with himself and his own fruition.

Bombay, 7th Public Talk, March 9, 1955
Collected Works, Vol. VIII, p. 339

Chastity can exist only when there is love, and without love there is no chastity.

Questioner: Is continence or chastity necessary for the attainment of liberation?

KRISHNAMURTI: The question is wrongly put. For the attainment of liberation, nothing is necessary. You cannot attain it through bargaining, through sacrifice, through elimination; it is not a thing that you can buy. If you do these things, you will get a thing of the marketplace, therefore not real. Truth cannot be bought, there is no means to truth; if there were a means, the end would not be truth, because means and end are one, they are not separate. Chastity as a means to liberation, to truth, is a denial of truth. Chastity is not a coin with which you buy it. You cannot buy truth with any coin, and you cannot buy chastity with any coin. You can buy only those things which you know, but you cannot buy truth because you don't know it. Truth comes into being only when the mind is quiet, still; so the problem is entirely different, is it not?

Why do we think chastity is essential? Why has sex become a problem? That is really the question, isn't it? We shall understand what it is to be chaste when we understand this corroding problem of sex. Let us find out why sex has become such an extremely important factor in our life— more of a problem than property, money, and so on. What do we mean by sex? Not merely the act, but thinking about it, feeling about it, anticipating it, escaping from it—that is our problem. Our problem is sensation, wanting more and more. Watch yourself, don't watch your neighbor. Why are your thoughts so occupied with sex. Chastity can exist only when there is love, and without love there is no chastity. Without love, chastity is merely lust in a different form. To become chaste is to become something else; it is like a man becoming powerful, succeeding as a prominent lawyer, politician, or whatever else—the change is on the same level. That is not chastity, but merely the end result of a dream, the outcome of the continual resistance to a particular desire. So, our problem is not how to become chaste or to find out what are the things necessary for liberation, but to understand this problem which we call sex. Because, it is an enormous problem, and you cannot approach it with condemnation or justification. Of course, you can easily isolate yourself from it, but then you will be creating another problem. This all-important, engrossing, and destructive problem of sex can be understood only when the mind liberates itself from its own anchorage. Please think it out, don't brush it aside. As long as you are bound through fear, through tradition, to any particular job, activity, belief, idea, as long as you are conditioned by and attached to all that, you will have this problem of sex. Only when the mind is free of fear is there the fathomless, the inexhaustible, and only then does this problem take its ordinary place. Then you can deal with it simply and effectively; then it is not a problem. So, chastity ceases to be a problem where there is love. Then life is not a problem; life is to be lived completely in the fullness of love, and that revolution will bring about a new world.

Colombo, 2nd Public Talk, Ceylon, January 1, 1950
Collected Works, Vol. VI, pp. 56-7

A disciplined heart, a suppressed heart, cannot know what love is.

Those who are trying to be celibate in order to achieve God are unchaste for they are seeking a result or gain and so substituting the end, the result, for sex—which is fear. Their hearts are without love, and there can be no purity, and a pure heart alone can find reality. A disciplined heart, a suppressed heart, cannot know what love is. It cannot know love if it is caught in habit, in sensation—religious or physical, psychological or sensate. The idealist is an imitator and therefore he cannot know love. He cannot be generous, give himself over completely without the thought of himself. Only when the mind and heart are unburdened of fear, of the routine of sensational habits, when there is generosity and compassion, there is love. Such love is chaste.

Bombay, 5th Public Talk, February 15, 1948
Collected Works, Vol. IV, p. 177

We have never said that love and sex are two separate things. We have said that love is whole, not to be broken up.

That morning the river was tarnished silver, for it was cloudy and cold. The leaves were covered with dust, and everywhere there was a thin layer of it—in the room, on the veranda and on the chair. It was getting colder; it must have snowed heavily in the Himalayas; one could feel the biting wind from the north, even the birds were aware of it. But the river that morning had a strange movement of its own; it didn't seem to be ruffled by the wind, it seemed almost motionless and had that timeless quality which all waters seem to have. How beautiful it was! No wonder people have made it into a sacred river. You could sit there, on that veranda, and meditatively watch it endlessly. You weren't day-dreaming; your thoughts weren't in any direction—they were simply absent.

And as you watched the light on that river, somehow you seemed to lose yourself, and as you closed your eyes there was a penetration into a void that was full of blessing. This was bliss.

He came again that morning, with a young man. He was the monk who had talked about discipline, sacred books, and the authority of tradition. His face was freshly washed, and so were his robes. The young man seemed rather nervous. He had come with the monk, who was probably his guru, and was waiting for him to speak first. He looked at the river but he was thinking of other things. Presently the sannyasi said, "I have come again, but this time to talk about love and sensuality. We, who have taken the vow of chastity, have our sensuous problems. The vow is only a means of resisting our uncontrollable desires. I am an old man now, and these desires no longer burn me. Before I took the vows I was married. My wife died, and I left my home and went through a period of agony, of intolerable biological urges; I fought them night and day. It was a very difficult time, full of loneliness, frustration, fears of madness, and neurotic outbursts. Even now I daren't think about it too much. And this young man has come with me because I think he is going through the same problem. He wants to give up the world and take the vow of poverty and chastity, as I did. I have been talking to him for many weeks, and I thought it might be worthwhile if we could both talk over this problem with you, this problem of sex and love. I hope you don't mind if we talk quite frankly."

If we are going to concern ourselves with this matter, first, if we may suggest it, don't start to examine from a position, or an attitude, or a principle, for this will prevent you from exploration. If you are against sex, or if you insist that it is necessary to life, that it is a part of living, any such assumption will prevent real perception. We should put away any conclusion, and so be free to look, to examine.

There were a few drops of rain now, and the birds had become quiet, for it was going to rain heavily, and the leaves once again would be fresh and green, full of light and color.

There was a smell of rain, and the strange quietness that comes before a storm was on the land.

So we have two problems—love and sex. The one is an abstract idea, the other is an actual daily biological urge—a fact that exists and cannot be denied. Let us first find out what love is, not as an abstract idea but what it actually is. What is it? Is it merely a sensuous delight, cultivated by thought as pleasure, the remembrance of an experience which has given great delight or sexual enjoyment? Is it the beauty of a sunset, or the delicate leaf that you touch or see, or the perfume of the flower that you smell? Is love pleasure, or desire? Or is it none of these? Is love to be divided as the sacred and the profane? Or is it something indivisible, whole, that cannot be broken up by thought? Does it exist without the object? Or does it come into being only because of the object? Is it because you see the face of a woman that love arises in you—love then being sensation, desire, pleasure, to which thought gives continuity? Or is love a state in you which responds to beauty as tenderness? Is love something cultivated by thought so that its object becomes important, or is it utterly unrelated to thought and, therefore, independent, free? Without understanding this word and the meaning behind it we shall be tortured, or become neurotic about sex, or be enslaved by it.

Love is not to be broken up into fragments by thought. When thought breaks it up into fragments, as impersonal, personal, sensuous, spiritual, my country and your country, my god and your god, then it is no longer love, then it is something entirely different—a product of memory, of propaganda, of convenience, of comfort, and so on.

Is sex the product of thought? Is sex—the pleasure, the delight, the companionship, the tenderness involved in it—is this a remembrance strengthened by thought? In the sexual act there is self-forgetfulness, self-abandonment, a sense of the non-existence of fear, anxiety, the worries of life. Remembering this state of tenderness and self-forgetfulness, and demanding its repetition, you chew over it, as it were, until the next occasion. Is this tenderness, or is it merely a recollection of something that is over and which, through repetition, you hope to capture again? Is not the repetition of something, however pleasurable, a destructive process?

The young man suddenly found his tongue: "Sex is a biological urge, as you yourself have said, and if this is destructive then isn't eating equally destructive, because that also is a biological urge?"

If one eats when one is hungry—that is one thing. If one is hungry and thought says: "I must have the taste of this or that type of food"—then it is thought, and it is this which is the destructive repetition.

"In sex, how do you know what is the biological urge, like hunger, and what is a psychological demand, like greed?" asked the young man.

Why do you divide the biological urge and the psychological demand? And there is yet another question, a different question altogether—why do you separate sex from seeing the beauty of a mountain or the loveliness of a flower? Why do you give such tremendous importance to the one and totally neglect the other?

"If sex is something quite different from love, as you seem to say, then is there any necessity at all to do anything about sex?" asked the young man.

We have never said that love and sex are two separate things. We have said that love is whole, not to be broken up, and thought, by its very nature, is fragmentary. When thought dominates, obviously there is no love. Man generally knows—perhaps only knows—the sex of thought, which is the chewing of the cud of pleasure and its repetition. Therefore we have to ask: Is there any other kind of sex which is not of thought or desire?

The sannyasi had listened to all this with quiet attention. Now he spoke: "I have resisted it, I have taken a vow against it, because by tradition, by reason, I have seen that one must have energy for the religious dedicated life. But I now see that this resistance has taken a great deal of energy. I have spent more time on resisting, and wasted more energy on it, than I have ever wasted on sex itself. So what you have said—that a conflict of any kind is a waste of energy—I now understand. Conflict and struggle are far more deadening than the seeing of a woman's face, or even perhaps than sex itself."

Is there love without desire, without pleasure? Is there sex, without desire, without pleasure? Is there love which is whole, without thought entering into it? Is sex something of the past, or is it something each time new? Thought is obviously old, so we are always contrasting the old and the new. We are asking questions from the old, and we want an answer in terms of the old. So when we ask: Is there sex without the whole mechanism of thought operating and working, doesn't it mean that we have not stepped out of the old? We are so conditioned by the old that we do not feel our way into the new. We said love is whole, and always new—new not as opposed to the old, for that again is the old. Any assertion that there is sex without desire is utterly valueless, but if you have followed the whole meaning of thought, then perhaps you will come upon the other. If, however, you demand that you must have your pleasure at any price, then love will not exist.

The young man said: "That biological urge you spoke about is precisely such a demand, for though it may be different from thought, it engenders thought."

"Perhaps I can answer my young friend," said the sannyasi, "for I have been through all this. I have trained myself for years not to look at a woman. I have ruthlessly controlled the biological demand. The biological urge does not engender thought; thought captures it, thought utilizes it, thought makes images, pictures out of this urge—and then the urge is a slave to thought. It is thought which engenders the urge so much of the time. As I said, I am beginning to see the extraordinary nature of our own deception and dishonesty. There is a great deal of hypocrisy in us. We can never see things as they are but must create illusions about them. What you are telling us, sir, is to look at everything with clear eyes, without the memory of yesterday; you have repeated this so often in your talks. Then life does not become a problem. In my old age I am just beginning to realize this."

The young man looked not completely satisfied. He wanted life according to *his* terms, according to the formula which he had carefully built.

This is why it is very important to know oneself, not according to any formula or according to any guru. This constant choiceless awareness ends all illusions and all hypocrisy.

Now it was coming down in torrents, and the air was very still, and there was only the sound of the rain on the roof and on the leaves.

Second Penguin Krishnamurti Reader, pp. 72-7

The effort that has gone into suppression, into control, into this denial of your desire, distorts your mind.

Most of us spend our life in effort, in struggle; and the effort, the struggle, the striving, is a dissipation of that energy. Man, throughout the historical period of man, has said that to find that reality or God—whatever name he may give to it—you must be a celibate, that is, you take a vow of chastity and suppress, control, battle with yourself endlessly all your life, to keep your vow. Look at the waste of energy! It is also a waste of energy to indulge. And it has far more significance when you suppress. The effort that has gone into suppression, into control, into this denial of your desire, distorts your mind, and through that distortion you have a certain sense of austerity which becomes harsh. Please listen. Observe it in yourself and observe the people around you. And observe this waste of energy, the battle. Not the implications of sex, not the actual act, but the ideals, the images, the pleasure—the constant thought about them is a waste of energy. And most people waste their energy either through denial, or through a vow of chastity, or in thinking about it endlessly.

Bombay, 7th Public Talk, March 3, 1965
Collected Works, Vol. XV, pp. 89-90

If there is disorder in my life in regard to sex, then the rest of my life is in disorder. So I shouldn't ask how to put one corner in order, but why I have broken life into so many different fragments . . .

Questioner: Many years ago, when I first became interested in the so-called religious life, I made the strong resolve to cut out sex altogether. I conformed rigorously to what I considered to be an essential requirement of that life and lived with all the fierce austerity of a monkish celibate. Now I see that that kind of puritanical conformity in which suppression and violence are involved is stupid, yet I don't want to go back to my old life. How am I to act now in regard to sex?

KRISHNAMURTI: Why is it that you don't know what to do when there is desire? I'll tell you why. Because this rigid decision of yours is still in operation. All religions have told us to deny sex, to suppress it, because they say it is a waste of energy and you must have energy to find God. But this kind of austerity and harsh suppression and conformity to a pattern does brutal violence to all our finer instincts. This kind of harsh austerity is a greater waste of energy than indulgence in sex.

Why have you made sex into a problem? Really it doesn't matter at all whether you go to bed with someone or whether you don't. Get on with it or drop it, but don't make a problem of it. The problem comes from this constant preoccupation. The really interesting thing is not whether we do or don't go to bed with someone but why we have all these fragments in our lives. In one restless corner there is sex with all its preoccupations; in another corner there is some other kind of turmoil; in another a striving after this or that, and in each corner there is the continual chattering of the mind. There are so many ways in which energy is wasted.

If one corner of my life is in disorder, then the whole of my life is in disorder. If there is disorder in my life in regard to sex, then the rest of my life is in disorder. So I shouldn't ask how to put one corner in order, but why I have broken life into so many different fragments—fragments which are in disorder within themselves and which all contradict each other. What can I do when I see so many fragments? How can I deal with them all? I have these fragments because I am not whole inside. If I go into all this without causing yet another fragment, if I go to the very end of each fragment, then in that awareness, which is looking, there is no fragmentation. Each fragment is a separate pleasure. I should ask myself whether I am going to stay in some sordid little room of pleasure all my life. Go into the slavery of each pleasure, each fragment, and say to yourself, my god, I am dependent, I am a slave to all these little corners—is that all there is to my life? Stay with it and see what happens.

Meeting Life, pp. 61-2

When we see this whole picture, not as an idea but as an actual act, then love, sex, and chastity are one.

When we see this whole thing—what we make of love, of sex, of self-indulgence, of taking vows against it—when we see this whole picture, not as an idea but as an actual fact, then love, sex and chastity are one. They are not separate. It is the separation in relationship that corrupts. Sex can be as chaste as the blue sky without a cloud; but the cloud comes and darkens, with thought. Thought says: "This is chaste, and this is indulgence," "This must be controlled," and "In this I will let myself go." So thought is the poison, not love, not chastity, not sex.

That which is innocent, whatever it does, is always chaste; but innocence is not the product of thought.

Conversations, pp. 12-13

VI. On Marriage

One has to find out how to live with another . . . without any sense of struggle, adaptation, or adjustment.

KRISHNAMURTI: When two people live together, is it a sexual, biological activity of coming together, or is there love in their lives, caring for each other? Perhaps you know this answer better than the speaker.

Questioner: Is it necessary to marry in love? What is the physical relationship between man and woman?

KRISHNAMURTI: I don't know, you ought to know. What a strange question this is, isn't it? Is it necessary to marry in love? What do you say? If the speaker puts this question to you, what will you answer: Is it necessary, sirs and ladies, that I should marry? What would be your answer? Your answer would probably be: Do what you want to do, why bother me with it; it's up to you.

But you see the question is really much more complex than that. We all want companionship, we all want sexual relationships, a biological necessity. And also we want somebody on whom we can rely, in whom we can find security, in whom there is a sense of comfort, support. Because most of us cannot stand alone, on our own feet, therefore we say, I must marry, or I will have a friend, or whatever it is, I must have somebody with whom

I can be at home. We are never at home with anybody because we are living in our own thoughts, in our own problems, in our own ambitions, and so on. We are frightened to stand alone. Because life is very lonely, life is very, very complex and troublesome and one needs somebody with whom you can talk things over. Also, when you marry you have a sexual relationship, children, and so on. In this relationship between man and woman, if there is no love, you use her and she uses you, you exploit her and she exploits you. That's a fact.

So the questioner asks, what is the physical relationship between man and woman. Don't you know? It's up to you, sirs. But to really enter into this whole complex problem of living together—not only two people, but living together with humanity, with your neighbour, with your boss, with your servant (if you have a servant), with your father and mother and children—it's a very complex thing. Living together as a family gives you a certain security, certain safety, and so you extend that family to a group, to a community, to a state, to a nation. And from that to a nation which is opposed to another nation, and so there is always division and conflict, and wars.

So one has to find out how to live with another without any conflict, without any sense of struggle, adaptation, adjustment. That requires a great deal of intelligence, integrity. But we just marry because of sexual, biological demands, and so on.

Bombay, February 9, 1984

Questioner: Most of us are married, or involved in a close relationship which began for all the wrong reasons you have so correctly described. Can such a marriage or relationship ever be made into a really positive force? [Laughter]

KRISHNAMURTI: You poor chaps! Now, how do we tackle this question? What does it mean to be related to another? You may be related very closely, intimately, physically, but are we ever related psychologically, inwardly? Not romantically, sentimentally, but the feeling of being related? The word *relation* means to be in contact, to have a sense of wholeness with another, not as separate entities coming together and feeling whole, but the very relationship brings about this quality, this feeling of not being separate. This is really quite an important question because most of our lives are so terribly isolated, insulated, carefully structured so that we are not psychologically disturbed. And such relationship will inevitably bring about conflict, disturbance, and all the neurotic behavior that one has. So first, let's be clear together what we mean by relationship, not only the meaning of that word, the verbal meaning, but the significance that lies behind the word, behind the two people.

What does it mean to be related? Are we ever related in the deep profound sense of that word? Can there be a relationship of that kind, undisturbed like the depth of the sea? Can there be a relationship if each one of us is pursuing his own particular path, particular desire, particular ambition, and so on? Can there be such relationship with the other if these things exist? You say, "How can they not exist? Is it not necessary for each one of us to fulfill, each one of us to flower with each other?" What does that mean when that sense of separateness exists? If each of us says we are helping each other to flower, to grow, to fulfill, to be happy together, then one is still maintaining the isolated spirit. Now, why does the mind or the brain, the human entity, always cling to separatism?

Please, this is a very, very serious question: Why have human beings throughout history maintained this sense of isolation, insulation, separatism, division? You are a Catholic, I am a Protestant. You belong to that group, and he belongs to that group. I put on a purple robe, or a yellow robe, or a garland round me, and we maintain this—and we talk about relationship, love, and all the rest of it. Now, why? Please, we are co-operating, investigating together. Why do we do this? Is it conscious and deliberate, or unconscious, tradition, our education? The whole religious structure maintains that you are separate, separate souls, and so on. Is it that thought in itself is separative? You understand? I think I am separate from you. I think my behavior must be separate from yours, because otherwise there is the fear that we will become automatic, zombies, imitating each other. Is thought the cause of this separatism in life? Please investigate together in this. Thought has separated the world into nationalities. You are British, another is German; I am French, you are Russian, and so on. This division is created by thought. And thought assumes that in this separatism, in this division, there is security—belonging to a commune, belonging to the same group, believing in the same guru, believing in the same clothes that one wears according to the edicts of the guru—one feels secure, has at least the illusion of being secure.

And so we are asking: Is it pleasure, the pleasurable desire, which is also the movement of thought, that separates us? Right? That is, is thought ever complete, whole? Because thought is based on knowledge, which is vast accumulated experience of man, either in the scientific, technological world, or psychologically. We have accumulated a great deal of knowledge, outwardly and inwardly. And thought is the outcome of that knowledge—thought as memory, knowledge, experience. So, knowledge can never be complete about anything—about God, about *nirvana,* about heaven, about science, anything. So, knowledge must always go with the shadow of ignorance. Please see this fact together. So when thought enters into the field of relationship it must create a division, because thought itself is fragmented, thought itself is limited—right?

If this is clear to all of us—I am not explaining, you are discovering it for yourselves—then what place has knowledge in relationship? Please, this is a serious question, it isn't just a casual, argumentative proposition. This is an enquiry into what place has knowledge, experience, accumulated memories, in relationship. Please answer this yourself, don't look at me. If I say, "I know my wife"—or another form of intimate relationship—I have already put that person into the framework of my knowledge about her or him. So my knowledge becomes the divisive process. I have lived with my wife, husband, girl, or whatever it is, and I have accumulated information. I have remembered the painful statements she has made or one has made, there is this whole building up of memory as an image, which interferes in my relationship with another. Right? Please observe this in yourself. And she is doing exactly the same thing. So we are asking: what place has knowledge in relationship? Is knowledge love? I may know my wife—the way she looks, the way she behaves, certain habits, and so on. That is fairly obvious. But why should I say, "I know her"? When I say, "I know" I have already limited my relationship. I don't know if you understand? I have already created a block, a barrier between myself and her. Does that mean in my relationship to her I become irresponsible? You understand my question? If I say, "I don't know you basically", am I irresponsible? Or have I become extraordinarily sensitive—if I may use that word; that is a wrong word—I am vulnerable, I have no sense of division, no barrier.

So if I have this quality of mind, brain, or feeling that relationship is a flowering, a movement—it is not a static state, it is a living thing, you can't put it in a crate and say that is it, and not move from there—then we can begin to ask: What is marriage? Right? Or, not marriage; one may live with another, sexually, as companions, holding hands, talking, and go to a Registrar, or go through a Catholic or Protestant ceremony and be tied together, or I may live with another without being married. With one I have taken a vow of responsibility; in the other I don't. With one I am legally married, separation or divorce becomes rather difficult; with the other it is fairly simple, we each say goodbye and walk off in different directions. And that is what is happening more and more in the world. We are not condemning either. Please, we are just looking at this whole problem: the responsibility and the feeling of the tremendous burden of children. And there, legally, you are tied; in the other you are not, you may have children but there is always this open door.

Now, is all relationship in both these cases a mere form of attraction, biological responses on both sides, curiosity, the sense of wanting to be with another—which may be the outcome of unconscious fear of loneliness, the tradition which has established this habit? In both cases it can become a habit, and in both cases there is the fear of losing, possessing, exploiting each other sexually, and all the rest that follows. Now, in both cases, what is important? Please, we are talking over together; I am not telling you what is or what is not. What is important, necessary in both cases? Responsibility is essential—right? I am responsible for the people I live with. I am responsible, not only with my wife, but I am responsible for what is happening in the world. I am responsible to see that people are not killed. I am responsible. I am responsible to see that there is no violence. Right?

So is my responsibility just for the one and for my family, for my children, which has been the tradition? In the West, the family is disappearing more and more; whereas, in the East, the family is still the center. It is tremendously important; for the family they will do anything; even though they are distant cousins they will keep together, help each other, pull wires for each other. But here it is gradually disappearing altogether.

You see, sirs, when you go into this problem it becomes extraordinarily complex and extraordinarily vital. If I have children, if I love them as I do and I feel responsible, I am responsible for the whole of their lives, and they must be responsible for me for the whole of their life. I must see that they are properly educated, not butchered by war.

So, all that is implied in this question. Investigating it profoundly, one sees that, unless one has this quality of love, everything is just beside the point. And if I am attempting not to be self-centered, not to be isolated, to have this feeling of deep affection in which there is no attachment, no possession, not the pursuit of pleasure, and my wife feels the opposite, then we have a totally different problem. You understand this? Then the problem is: What shall I do? Just leave her, run away, divorce. I may have to if she insists. It is not a question to be answered by a few statements but it requires a great deal of inward inquiry into this on both parts. And in that inquiry, in exploring, if there is no love then there is no intelligent action. Where there is love it has its own intelligence, its own responsibility.

Brockwood Park, England, September 2, 1982

When you love your wife . . . you do not dominate.

In this country, a husband is the boss; he is the law, the master, because he is economically dominant, and it is he who says what the duties of a wife are. Since the wife is not dominant and is economically dependent, what she says are not duties. We can approach the problem from the point of view of the husband, or of the wife. If we approach the problem of the wife, we see that because she is not free economically, her education is limited, or her thinking capacities may be inferior; and society has imposed upon her regulations and modes of conduct determined by the men. Therefore, she accepts what are called the rights of the husband; and as he is dominant, being economically free, and has the capacity to earn, he lays down the law. Naturally, where marriage is a matter of contract, there is no limit to its complications. Then there is *duty*—a bureaucratic word that has no significance in relationship. When one establishes regulations and begins to inquire into the duties and rights of husband and wife, there is no end to it. Surely, such a relationship is an appalling affair, is it not? When the husband demands his rights and insists on having a dutiful wife, whatever that may mean, their relationship is obviously merely a business contract. It is very important to understand this question, for surely, there must be a different approach to it. As long as relationship is based on contract, on money, on possession, authority, or domination, then inevitably relationship becomes a matter of rights and duties. One can see the extreme complexity of relationship when it is the result of a contract—determining what is right, what is wrong, what is duty. If I am the wife and you insist on certain actions, not being independent, naturally I have to succumb to your wishes, your holding the reins. You impose on the wife certain regulations, rights, and duties, and therefore relationship becomes merely a matter of contract, with all its complexities.

Now, is there not a different approach to this problem? That is, when there is love, there is no duty. When you love your wife, you share everything with her—your property, your trouble, your anxiety, your joy. You do not dominate. You are not the man and she the woman to be used and thrown aside, a sort of breeding machine to carry on your name. When there is love, the word *duty* disappears. It is the man with no love in his heart who talks of rights and duties, and in this country duties and rights have taken the place of love. Regulations have become more important than the warmth of affection. When there is love, the problem is simple; when there is no love, the problem becomes complex. When a man loves his wife and his children, he can never possibly think in terms of *duty* and *rights*. Sirs, examine your own hearts and minds. I know you laugh it off—that is one of the tricks of the thoughtless, to laugh at something and push it aside. Your wife does not share your responsibility, your wife does not share your property, she does not have the half of everything that you have because you consider the woman less than yourself, something to be kept and to be used sexually at your convenience when your appetite demands it. So you have invented the words *rights* and *duty;* and when the woman rebels, you throw at her these words. It is a static society, a deteriorating society, that talks of duty and rights. If you really examine your hearts and minds, you will find that you have no love.

For a new society, a new culture to come into being, obviously there cannot be domination either by the man or by the woman. Domination exists because of inward poverty. Being psychologically poor, we want to dominate, to swear at the servant, at the wife or husband. Surely, it is the sense of affection, that warmth of love, which alone can bring about a new state, a new culture. The cultivation of the heart is not a process of the mind. The mind cannot cultivate the heart, but when the process of the mind is understood, then love comes into being. Love is not a mere word. The word is not the thing; the word *love* is not love. When we use that word and try to cultivate love, it is merely a process of the mind. Love cannot be cultivated, but when we realize that the word is not the thing, then the mind, with its laws and regulations, with its rights and duties, ceases to interfere, and then only is there a possibility of creating a new culture, a new hope, and a new world.

Poona, 3rd Public Talk, India, September 12, 1948
Collected Works, Vol. V, pp. 87-8

Marriage as a habit, as a cultivation of habitual pleasure, is a deteriorating factor, because there is no love in habit.

It is only for the very, very few who love that the married relationship has significance, and then it is unbreakable; then it is not mere habit or convenience, nor is it based on biological, sexual need. In that love which is unconditional, the identities are fused, and in such a relationship there is a remedy, there is hope.

But for most of you, the married relationship is not fused. To fuse the separate identities, you have to know yourself, and she has to know herself. That means, to love. But there is no love, which is an obvious fact. Love is fresh, new, not mere gratification, not mere habit: it is unconditional. You don't treat your husband or wife that way, do you? You live in your isolation, and she lives in her isolation, and you have established your habits of assured sexual pleasure. What happens to a man who has an assured income? Surely, he deteriorates. Have you not noticed it? Watch a man who has an assured income and you will soon see how rapidly his mind is withering away. He may have a big position, a reputation for cunning, but the full joy of life is gone out of him.

Similarly, you have a marriage in which you have a permanent source of pleasure, a habit without understanding, without love, and you are forced to live in that state. I am not saying what you should do, but look at the problem first. Do you think that is right? It does not mean that you must throw off your wife and pursue someone else. What does this relationship mean? Surely, to love is to be in communion with somebody, but are you in communion with your wife, except physically? Do you know her, except physically? Does she know you? Are you not both isolated, each pursuing his or her own interests, ambitions, and needs, each seeking from the other gratification, economic or psychological security? Such a relationship is not a relationship at all—it is a mutually self-enclosing process of psychological, biological, and economic necessity—and the obvious result is conflict, misery, nagging, possessive fear, jealousy, and so on.

So, marriage as a habit, as a cultivation of habitual pleasure, is a deteriorating factor because there is no love in habit. Love is not habitual; love is something joyous, creative, new. Therefore, habit is the contrary of love, but you are caught in habit, and naturally your habitual relationship with another is dead. So, we come back again to the fundamental issue, which is that the reformation of society depends on you, not on legislation. Legislation can only make for further habit or conformity;

therefore, you, as a responsible individual in relationship, have to do something—you have to act, and you can act only when there is an awakening of your mind and heart. I see some of you nodding your heads in agreement with me, but the obvious fact is that you don't want to take the responsibility for transformation, for change; you don't want to face the upheaval of finding out how to live rightly. And so the problem continues; you quarrel and carry on, and finally you die, and when you die somebody weeps, not for the other fellow, but for his or her own loneliness. You carry on unchanged, and you think you are human beings capable of legislation, of occupying high positions, talking about God, finding a way to stop wars, and so on. None of these things mean anything because you have not solved any of the fundamental issues.

New Delhi, 3rd Public Talk, India, December 19, 1948
Collected Works, Vol. V, pp. 175-6

Questioner: If two people have a relationship of conflict and pain, can they resolve it, or must the relationship end? To have a good relationship isn't it necessary for both to change?

KRISHNAMURTI: I hope the question is clear. What is the cause in relationship of pain, conflict, and all the problems that arise? What is the root of it? Please, in answering these questions we are thinking together. I am not answering for you just to receive or accept or reject, but together we are inquiring into these questions. This is a question that concerns all human beings whether they are in the East, here, or in America. This is a problem that really concerns most human beings. Apparently two people, man and woman, cannot live together without conflict, without pain, without a sense of inequality, without that feeling that they are not profoundly related to each other. One asks why? There may be multiple causes: sex, temperament, opposite feelings, belief, ambition. There may be many, many causes for this lack of harmony in relationship. But what is really the source, the depth of that source, that brings conflict in each of us? I think that is the important question to ask, and then do not wait for an answer from somebody, like the speaker, but having put the question, have the patience to wait, hesitate, let the question itself take seed, flower, move. I don't know if I am conveying that feeling to you.

I ask myself why, if I am married to a woman, or live with a woman, why do I have this basic conflict between us? I can give a superficial answer—because she is a Roman Catholic and I am a Protestant, or this or that. Those are all superficial reasons, but I want to find out what is the deep root, or deep source of this conflict between two people. I have put the question, and I am waiting for the question itself to flower, to expose all the intricacies in the question and what the question brings out. For that, I must have a little patience—right?—a little sense of waiting, watching, being aware, so that the question begins to unfold. As it unfolds I begin to see the answer. Not that I want an answer, but the question itself begins to unroll, show me the extraordinary complexity that lies between two people, between two human beings that perhaps like each other, perhaps are attracted to each other. When they are very young they get sexually involved, and so on, and later as they grow a little older they get bored with each other and gradually escape from that boredom through another person, divorcing—you know all the rest of it. But they find the same problem with another. So I have to have patience. By that word *patience* I mean not allowing time to operate. I do not know if you have gone into the question of patience and impatience.

Most of us are rather impatient. We want our question answered immediately, or we want to escape from it immediately, to operate upon it immediately. So we are rather impatient to get on with it. This impatience doesn't give one the depth of understanding of the problem. Whereas if I have patience, which is not of time, I am not wanting to end the problem; I am watching, looking at the problem, letting it evolve, grow. So out of that patience I begin to find out the depth of the answer. Right? Let us do that together now. We are patient, not wanting an immediate answer, and therefore our minds, brains are open to look, are aware of the problem and its complexity. Right? We are trying—no, I don't want to use the word *trying*—we are penetrating into the problem of why two people can never seem to live together without conflict. What is the root of this conflict? What is my relationship with her, or with somebody? Is it superficial? That is, sexual attraction, the curiosity, the excitement, are all superficial sensory responses. Right? So I realize these responses are superficial, and as long as I try to find an answer superficially I will never be able to see the depth of the problem. So, am I free from the superficial responses, and the problems that superficial responses create, and the attempt to solve those problems superficially? I don't know if you are following?

I have seen that I won't find an answer superficially; therefore, I ask what the root of it is. Is it education? Is it that, being a man, I want to dominate the other, that I want to possess the other? Am I attached so deeply I don't want to let go? And do I see that being tied, attached, will invariably bring about corruption—corruption in the sense that I am jealous, I am anxious, I am frightened? One knows very well all the consequences of attachment. Is that the cause of it? Or is the cause much deeper? First of all, we said, superficial, then emotional, attachment, emotional and sentimental and romantic dependence. If I discard those, then is there still a deeper issue involved in this? Are you getting it? We are moving from the superficial, lower and deeper and deeper so that we can find out for ourselves what the root of it is. I hope you are doing this.

Now, how do I find the root of it? How do you find the root of it? Are you wanting an answer, wanting to find the root of it and therefore making a tremendous effort? Or you want to find it so your mind, your brain is quiet? It is looking, so it is not agitated, it is not the activity of desire, will. It is just watching. Are we doing together this, just watching to see what is the deep root, or deep cause, the basis of this conflict between human beings. Is it the sense of individual separation? See, go into it very carefully please. Is it individual concept that I am separate from the other basically? Biologically we are different, but there is the sense of deep-rooted individual separative action; is that the root of it? Or is there still a deeper root, a deeper layer—you understand? I wonder if you are following all this? We are together in this? First, sensory responses, sensual responses, then emotional, romantic, sentimental responses, then attachment, with all its corruption? Or is it something profoundly conditioned, a brain that says, "I am an individual, and he, or she, is an individual, and we are separate entities; each must fulfill in his own way and therefore the separation is basic"? Is that so? Is it basic? Or have I been educated to that, that I am an individual and she, also an individual, must fulfill herself in her own way, and I must equally? So we have already started from the very beginning in these two separate directions. They may be running parallel together but never meeting; like two railway lines that never meet. And all I am doing is trying to meet, trying to live harmoniously, struggling: "Oh, darling you are so good"—you follow?—repeating, repeating, but never meeting. Right?

So, if that is the cause—and apparently it appears to be the cause—the root of it, is that separative existence of an individual a reality? Or, it is an illusion that I have been nourishing, cherishing, holding onto, without any validity behind it? If it has no validity, I must be quite sure, absolutely, irrevocably sure that it is an illusion and ask if the brain can break away from that illusion and realize we are all similar, psychologically. You follow? My consciousness is the consciousness of the rest of mankind; though biologically we differ, psychologically, our consciousness is similar in all human beings. If I once realize this, not intellectually but in depth, in my heart, in my blood, in my guts, then my relationship to another undergoes a radical change. Right? It's inevitable.

Now, the questioner asks: We are in conflict, must it end? If we battle with each other all day long, as most people do in this struggle, conflict—you know, the bitterness, the anger, the hatred, the repulsion—we bear it as long as we can and then comes the moment when we have to break. We know the familiar pattern of this. There are more and more divorces. And the questioner asks: What is one to do? If I am everlastingly in conflict with my wife and somehow I can't patch it over, must the relationship end? Or, do I understand basically the cause of this disruption, of this conflict, which is the sense of separate individuality, and having seen the illusory nature of it, I am therefore no longer pursuing the individual line. So then what takes place when I have perceived that and live it—not verbally maintain it, but actually live it—what is my relationship with the person, with the woman who still thinks in terms of the individual? You understand my question?

It is very interesting. Go into it. I see, or she sees—better put it onto her—she sees the foolishness, the absurdity, the illusory nature of the individual. She understands it, she feels it, and I don't because I am a male, I am more aggressive, more driving, and all the rest of that. So what takes place between us? She has comprehended that nature and I have not. She won't quarrel with me, ever. Right? She won't enter into that area at all but I am constantly pushing her, driving her and trying to pull her into that area. I am creating the conflict, not she. Have you understood how the whole thing has moved? Are you following all this? The whole thing has moved. There are now not two people quarrelling but only one. See what has taken place. And I, if I am at all sensitive, if I have real feeling for her, I begin to transform also because she is irrevocably there. You understand? She will not move out of that. See what happens. If two immovable objects meet, there is conflict. I don't know if you see. But if one is immovable, the lady, and I am movable, I naturally yield to that which is immovable. Right? I wonder if you understand this. This is very simple.

So the problem then is resolved, if one has real comprehension of relationship—without the image, which we went into previously. Then by her very presence, by her very vitality of actuality, she is going to transform me, help me. That is the answer. Got it?

Saanen, Switzerland, July 31, 1981
On Relationship, pp. 5-9

Can't you fall in love and not have a possessive relationship?

Questioner: Is it possible for a man and woman to live together, to have sex and children, without all the turmoil, bitterness, and conflict inherent in such a relationship? Is it possible for there to be freedom on both sides? I don't mean by freedom that the husband or wife should constantly be having affairs with someone else. People usually come together and get married because they fall in love, and in that there is desire, choice, pleasure, possessiveness, and tremendous drive. The very nature of this in-loveness is from the start filled with the seeds of conflict.

KRISHNAMURTI: Is it? Need it be? I very much question that. Can't you fall in love and not have a possessive relationship? I love someone and she loves me and we get married—that is all perfectly straightforward and simple, in that there is no conflict at all. (When I say we get married I might just as well say we decide to live together—don't let's get caught up in words.) Can't one have that without the other, without the tail, as it were, necessarily following? Can't two people be in love and both be so intelligent and so sensitive that there is freedom and absence of a center that makes for conflict? Conflict is not in the feeling of being in love; the feeling of being in love is utterly without conflict. There is no loss of energy in being in love. The loss of energy is in the tail, in everything that follows—jealousy, possessiveness, suspicion, doubt, the fear of losing that love, the constant demand for reassurance and security. Surely it must be possible to function in a sexual relationship with someone you love without the nightmare which usually follows. Of course it is.

Meeting Life, pp. 63-4

VII. What Is Love?

I realize that love cannot exist when there is jealousy; love cannot exist when there is attachment. Now, is it possible for me to be free of jealousy and attachment? I realize that I do not love. That is a fact. I am not going to deceive myself; I am not going to pretend to my wife that I love her. I do not know what love is. But I do know that I am jealous and I do know that I am terribly attached to her and that in attachment there is fear, there is jealousy, anxiety; there is a sense of dependence. I do not like to depend but I depend because I am lonely; I am shoved around in the office, in the factory and I come home and I want to feel comfort and companionship, to escape from myself. Now I ask myself: how am I to be free of this attachment? I am taking that just as an example.

At first, I want to run away from the question. I do not know how it is going to end up with my wife. When I am really detached from her my relationship to her may change. She might be attached to me and I might not be attached to her or to any other woman. But I am going to investigate. So I will not run away from what I imagine might be the consequence of being totally free of all attachment. I do not know what love is, but I see very clearly, definitely, without any doubt, that attachment to my wife means jealousy, possession, fear, anxiety, and I want freedom from all that. So I begin to enquire; I look for a method and I get caught in a system. Some guru says: "I will help you to be detached, do this and this; practice this and this." I accept what he says because I see the importance of being free and he promises me that if I do what he says I will have reward. But I see that way that I am looking for reward. I see how silly I am; wanting to be free and getting attached to a reward.

I do not want to be attached and yet I find myself getting attached to the idea that somebody, or some book, or some method, will reward me with freedom from attachment. So, the reward becomes an attachment. So I say: "Look what I have done; be careful, do not get caught in that trap." Whether it is a woman, a method, or an idea, it is still attachment. I am very watchful now for I have learned something; that is, not to exchange attachment for something else that is still attachment.

I ask myself, "What am I to do to be free of attachment?" What is my motive in wanting to be free of attachment? Is it not that I want to achieve a state where there is no attachment, no fear, and so on? And I suddenly realize that motive gives direction and that direction will dictate my freedom. Why have a motive? What is motive? A motive is a hope, or a desire, to achieve something. I see that I am attached to a motive. Not only my wife, not only my idea, the method, but my motive has become my attachment! So I am all the time functioning within the field of attachment—the wife, the method, and the motive to achieve something in the future. To all this I am attached. I see that it is a tremendously complex thing; I did not realize that to be free of attachment implied all this. Now, I see this as clearly as I see on a map the main roads, the side roads, and the villages; I see it very clearly. Then I say to myself: "Now, is it possible for me to be free of the great attachment I have for my wife and also of the reward which I think I am going to get and of my motive?" To all this I am attached. Why? Is it that I am insufficient in myself? Is it that I am very, very lonely and therefore seek to escape from that feeling of isolation—by turning to a woman, an idea, a motive—as if I must hold onto something? I see that it is so: I am lonely and escaping through attachment to something from that feeling of extraordinary isolation.

So, I am interested in understanding why I am lonely, for I see it is that which makes me attached. That loneliness has forced me to escape through attachment to this or to that, and I see that as long as I am lonely the sequence will always be this. What does it mean to be lonely? How does it come about? Is it instinctual, inherited, or is it brought about by my daily activity? If it is an instinct, if it is inherited, it is part of my lot; I am not to blame. But as I do not accept this, I question it and remain with the question. I am watching and I am not trying to find an intellectual answer. I am not trying to tell the loneliness what it should do, or what it is; I am watching for it to tell me. There is a watchfulness for the loneliness to reveal itself. It will not reveal itself if I run away; if I am frightened; if I resist it. So I watch it. I watch it so that no thought interferes. Watching is much more important than thought coming in. And because my whole energy is concerned with the observation of that loneliness, thought does not come in at all. The mind is being challenged and it must answer. Being challenged, it is in a crisis. In a crisis you have great energy, and that energy remains without being interfered with by thought. This is a challenge which must be answered.

I started out having a dialogue with myself. I asked myself, what is this strange thing called love; everybody talks about it, writes about it—all the romantic poems, pictures, sex, and all other areas of it? I ask: "Is there such a thing as love?" I see it does not exist when there is jealousy, hatred, fear. So, I am not concerned with love anymore; I am concerned with *what is:* my fear, my attachment. Why am I attached? I see that one of the reasons—I do not say it is the whole reason—is that I am desperately lonely, isolated. The older I grow, the more isolated I become. So I watch it. This is a challenge to find out, and because it is a challenge, all energy is there to respond. That is simple. If there is some catastrophe, an accident or whatever it is, it is a challenge, and I have the energy to meet it. I do not have to ask: "How do I get this energy?" When the house is on fire I have the energy to move, extraordinary energy. I do not sit back and say: "Well, I must get this energy" and then wait; the whole house will be burned by then.

So, there is this tremendous energy to answer the question: Why is there this loneliness? I have rejected ideas, suppositions, and theories that it is inherited, that it is instinctual. All that means nothing to me. Loneliness is *what is.* Why is there this loneliness which every human being, if he is at all aware, goes through, superficially or most profoundly? Why does it come into being? Is it that the mind is doing something which is bringing it about? I have rejected theories as to instinct and inheritance, and I am asking: Is the mind, the brain itself, bringing about this loneliness, this total isolation? Is the movement of thought doing this? Is the thought in my daily life creating this sense of isolation? In the office I am isolating myself because I want to become the top executive, therefore thought is working all the time isolating itself. I see that thought is all the time operating to make itself superior, the mind is working itself towards this isolation.

So, the problem then is: Why does thought do this? Is it the nature of thought to work for itself? Is it the nature of thought to create this isolation? Education brings about this isolation; it gives me a certain career, a certain specialization, and so, isolation. Thought, being fragmentary, being limited and time binding, is creating this isolation. In that limitation, it has found security, saying, "I have a special career in my life; I am a professor; I am perfectly safe." So my concern is then: Why does thought do it? Is it in its very nature to do this? Whatever thought does must be limited.

Now, the problem is: Can thought realize that whatever it does is limited, fragmented and therefore isolating, and that whatever it does will be thus? This is a very important point: Can thought itself *realize* its own limitations? Or, am I telling it that it is limited? This, I see, is very important to understand; this is the real essence of the matter. If thought realizes itself that it is limited, then there is no resistance, no conflict; it says, "I am that." But if I am telling it that it is limited, then I become separate from the limitation; then I struggle to overcome the limitation. Therefore, there is conflict and violence, not love.

So does thought realize of itself that it is limited? I have to find out. I am being challenged. Because I am challenged, I have great energy. Put it differently: does consciousness realize its content is itself? Or, is it that I have heard another say: "Consciousness is its content; its content makes up consciousness"? Therefore, I say, "Yes, it is so." Do you see the difference between the two? The latter, created by thought, is imposed by the 'me'. If I impose something on thought, then there is conflict. It is like a tyrannical government imposing on someone, but here that government is what I have created.

So I am asking myself: Has thought realized its own limitations? Or is it pretending to be something extraordinary, noble, divine?—which is nonsense, because thought is based on memory. I see that there must be clarity about this point: that there is no outside influence imposing on thought, saying it is limited. Then, because there is no imposition, there is no conflict; it simply realizes it is limited; it realizes that whatever it does—its worship of God, and so on—is limited, shoddy, petty—even though it has created marvelous cathedrals throughout Europe in which to worship.

So, there has been in my conversation with myself the discovery that loneliness is created by thought. Thought has now realized of itself that it is limited and so cannot solve the problem of loneliness. As it cannot solve the problem of loneliness, does loneliness exist? Thought has created this sense of loneliness, this emptiness, because it is limited, fragmentary, divided. And when it realizes this, loneliness is not; therefore, there is freedom from attachment. I have done nothing; I have watched the attachment, what is implied in it—greed, fear, loneliness, all that—and by tracing it, observing it, not analyzing it, but just looking, looking and looking, there is the discovery that thought has done all this. Thought, because it is fragmentary, has created this attachment. When it realizes this, attachment ceases. There is no effort made at all, for the moment there is effort, conflict is back again.

In love there is no attachment; if there is attachment there is no love. There has been the removal of the major factor, through negation, of what it is not, through the negation of attachment. I know what it means in my daily life: no remembrance of anything my wife, my girlfriend, or my neighbor did to hurt me; no attachment to any image thought has created about her—how she has bullied me, how she has given me comfort, how I have had pleasure sexually—all the different things of which the movement of thought has created images, attachment to those images has gone.

And there are other factors—must I go through all those step by step, one by one? Or is it all over? Must I go through, must I investigate—as I have investigated attachment, fear, pleasure, and the desire for comfort? I see that I do not have to go through all the investigation of all these various factors; I see it at one glance, I have captured it.

So, through negation of what is not love, love is. I do not have to ask what love is; I do not have to run after it. If I run after it, it is not love, it is a reward. So I have negated, I have ended, in that enquiry, slowly, carefully, without distortion, without illusion, everything that it is not—the other is.

Brockwood Park, England, August 30, 1977
A Dialogue With Oneself, pp. 3-9

VIII. Love in Relationship

Love in relationship is a purifying process, as it reveals the ways of the self.

How easy it is to destroy the thing we love! How quickly a barrier comes between us—a word, a gesture, a smile! Health, mood, and desire cast a shadow, and what was bright becomes dull and burdensome. Through usage we wear ourselves out, and that which was sharp and clear becomes wearisome and confused. Through constant friction, hope, and frustration, that which was beautiful and simple becomes fearful and expectant. Relationship is complex and difficult, and few can come out of it unscathed. Though we would like it to be static, enduring, continuous, relationship is a movement, a process which must be deeply and fully understood and not made to conform to an inner or outer pattern. Conformity, which is the social structure, loses its weight and authority only when there is love. Love in relationship is a purifying process as it reveals the ways of the self. Without this revelation, relationship has little significance.

But how we struggle against this revelation! The struggle takes many forms: dominance or subservience, fear or hope, jealousy or acceptance, and so on and on. The difficulty is that we do not love; and if we *do* love we want it to function in a particular way, we do not give it freedom. We love with our minds and not with our hearts. Mind can modify itself, but love cannot; mind can make itself invulnerable, but love cannot; mind can always withdraw, be exclusive, become personal or impersonal. Love is not to be compared and hedged about. Our difficulty lies in that which we *call* love, which is really of the mind. We fill our hearts with the things of the mind and so keep our hearts ever empty and expectant. It is the mind that clings, that is envious, that holds and destroys. Our life is dominated by the physical centers and by the mind. We do not love and let it alone, but crave to be loved; we give in order to receive, which is the generosity of the mind and not of the heart. The mind is ever seeking certainty, security; and can love be made certain by the mind? Can the mind—whose very essence is of time—catch love, which is its own eternity?

But even the love of the heart has its own tricks, for we have so corrupted our heart that it is hesitant and confused. It is this that makes life so painful and wearisome. One moment we think we have love, and the next it is lost: there comes an imponderable strength, not of the mind, whose sources may not be fathomed; this strength is again destroyed by the mind, for in this battle the mind seems invariably to be the victor. This conflict within ourselves is not to be resolved by the cunning mind or by the hesitant heart. There is no means, no way to bring this conflict to an end. The very search for a means is another urge of the mind to be the master, to put away conflict in order to be peaceful, to have love, to become something.

Our greatest difficulty is to be widely and deeply aware that there is no means to love as a desirable end of the mind. When we understand this really and profoundly, then there is a possibility of receiving something that is not of this world. Without the touch of that something, do what we will, there can be no lasting happiness in relationship. If you have received that benediction and I have not, naturally you and I will be in conflict. You may not be in conflict, but I will be; and in my pain and sorrow I cut myself off. Sorrow is as exclusive as pleasure, and until there is that love which is not of my making, relationship is pain. If there is the benediction of that love, you cannot but love me whatever I may be, for then you do not shape love according to my behavior.

Whatever tricks the mind may play, you and I are separate; though we may be in touch with each other at some points, integration is not with you, but within myself. This integration is not brought about by the mind at any time; it comes into being only when the mind is utterly silent, having reached the end of its own tether. Only then is there no pain in relationship.

Commentaries on Living, Series I, pp. 40-2

You cannot think about love.

If you observe, what makes us stale in our relationship is thinking, thinking, thinking, calculating, judging, weighing, adjusting ourselves; and the one thing which frees us from that is love, which is not a process of thought. You cannot think about love. You can think about the person whom you love, but you cannot think about love.

Banaras, 3rd Public Talk, India, February 6, 1949
Collected Works, Vol. V, p. 197

We do not know what love is . . .

We do not know what love is: we know pleasure; we know the lust, the pleasure that is derived from that and the fleeting happiness which is shrouded off with thought, with sorrow. We do not know what "to love" means. Love is not a memory; love is not a word; love is not the continuity of a thing that has given you pleasure. You may have relationship, you may say, "I love my wife"; but you don't love. If you love your wife, there is no jealousy, there is no dominance, there is no attachment.

We do not know what love is, because we do not know what beauty is—the beauty of a sunset, the cry of a child, the swift movement of the bird across the sky, all the exquisite colors of a sunset. You are totally unaware, insensitive to all that; therefore, you are also insensitive to life.

Bombay, 5th Public Talk, February 23, 1964
Collected Works, Vol. XIV, p. 153

Is love permanent?

An experience of pleasure makes us demand more of it, and *the more* is this urge to be secure in our pleasures. If we love someone, we want to be quite sure that that love is returned, and we seek to establish a relationship which we at least hope will be permanent. All our society is based on that relationship. But is there anything which is permanent? Is there? Is love permanent? Our constant desire is to make sensation permanent, is it not? And the thing which cannot be made permanent, which is love, passes us by.

London, 4th Public Talk, May 9, 1961
Collected Works, Vol. XII, p. 134

The state of love is not of the past or of the future.

I wonder if you have ever considered the nature of love? Loving is one thing, and having loved is another. Love has no time. You cannot say, "I have loved"—it has no meaning. Then love is dead, you do not love: the state of love is not of the past or of the future. Similarly, knowledge is one thing, and the movement of knowing is another. Knowledge is binding, but the movement of knowing is not binding.

Just feel your way into this, don't accept or deny it. You see, knowledge has the quality of time; it is time-bound, whereas the movement of knowing is timeless. If I want to know the nature of love, of meditation, of death, I cannot accept or deny anything. My mind must be in a state, not of doubt, but of inquiry—which means that it has no bondage to the past. The mind that is in the movement of knowing is free of time, because there is no accumulation.

Bombay, 3rd Public Talk, December 30, 1959
Collected Works, Vol. XI, p. 269

There is no division between man and woman when you love somebody.

Love is not of the mind, but since we have cultivated the mind, we use that word *love* to cover the field of the mind. Surely, love has nothing to do with the mind, it is not the product of the mind; love is entirely independent of calculation, of thought. When there is no love, then the framework of marriage as an institution becomes a necessity. When there is love, then sex is not a problem—it is the lack of love that makes it into a problem. Don't you know? When you love somebody really deeply—not with the love of the mind, but really from your heart—you share with him or her everything that you have, not your body only, but everything. In your trouble, you ask her help and she helps you. There is no division between man and woman when you love somebody, but there is a sexual problem when you do not know that love. We know only the love of the brain; thought has produced it, and a product of thought is still thought, it is not love.

Poona, India, 4th Public Talk, September 19, 1948
Collected Works, Vol. V, p. 99

Love comes into being when we understand the total process of ourselves.

Questioner: You have talked about relationship based on usage of another for one's own gratification, and you have often hinted at a state called love. What do you mean by love?

KRISHNAMURTI: We know what our relationship is: a mutual gratification and use, though we clothe it by calling it love. In usage there is tenderness for and the safeguarding of what is used. We safeguard our frontier, our books, our property; similarly, we are careful in safeguarding our wives, our families, our society, because without them we would be lonely, lost. Without the child, the parent feels lonely; what you are not, the child will be, so the child becomes an instrument of your vanity. We know the relationship of need and usage. We need the postman and he needs us, yet we don't say we love the postman. But we do say that we love our wives and children, even though we use them for our personal gratification and are willing to sacrifice them for the vanity of being called patriotic. We know this process very well, and obviously, it cannot be love. Love that uses, exploits, and then feels sorry, cannot be love because love is not a thing of the mind.

Now, let us experiment and discover what love is—discover, not merely verbally, but by actually experiencing that state. When you use me as a guru and I use you as disciples, there is mutual exploitation. Similarly, when you use your wife and children for your furtherance, there is exploitation. Surely, that is not love. When there is use, there must be possession; possession invariably breeds fear, and with fear come jealousy, envy, suspicion. When there is usage, there cannot be love, for love is not something of the mind. To think about a person is not to love that person. You think about a person only when that person is not present, when he is dead, when he has run off, or when he does not give you what you want. Then your inward insufficiency sets the process of the mind going. When that person is close to you, you do not think of him; to think of him when he is close to you is to be disturbed, so you take him for granted—he is there. Habit is a means of forgetting and being at peace so that you won't be disturbed. So, usage must invariably lead to invulnerability, and that is not love.

What is that state when usage—which is thought process as a means to cover the inward insufficiency, positively or negatively—is not? What is that state when there is no sense of gratification? Seeking gratification is the very nature of the mind. Sex is sensation which is created, pictured by the mind, and then the mind acts or does not act. Sensation is a process of thought, which is not love. When the mind is dominant and the thought process is important, there is no love. This process of usage, thinking, imagining, holding, enclosing, rejecting, is all smoke, and when the smoke is not, the flame of love is. Sometimes we do have that flame—rich, full, complete; but the smoke returns because we cannot live long with the flame, which has no sense of nearness, either of the one or the many, either personal or impersonal. Most of us have occasionally known the perfume of love and its vulnerability; but the smoke of usage, habit, jealousy, possession, the contract and the breaking of the contract—all these have become important for us, and therefore the flame of love is not. When the smoke is, the flame is not, but when we understand the truth of usage, the flame is. We use another because we are inwardly poor, insufficient, petty, small, lonely, and we hope that by using another, we can escape. Similarly, we use God as a means of escape. The love of God is not the love of truth. You cannot love truth; loving truth is only a means of using it to gain something else that you know, and therefore there is always the personal fear that you will lose something that you know.

You will know love when the mind is very still and free from its search for gratification and escapes. First, the mind must come entirely to an end. Mind is the result of thought, and thought is merely a passage, a means to an end. When life is merely a passage to something, how can there be love? Love comes into being when the mind is naturally quiet—not made quiet—when it sees the false as false and the true as true. When the mind is quiet, then whatever happens is the action of love, it is not the action of knowledge. Knowledge is mere experience, and experience is not love. Experience cannot know love. Love comes into being when we understand the total process of ourselves, and the understanding of ourselves is the beginning of wisdom.

Madras, 3rd Public Talk, February 5, 1950
Collected Works, Vol. VI, pp. 42-3

You flower only in relationship.

So you flower only in relationship; you flower only in love, not in contention. But our hearts are withered; we have filled our hearts with the things of the mind, and so we look to others to fill our minds with their creations. Since we have no love, we try to find it with the teacher, with someone else. Love is a thing that cannot be found. You cannot buy it, you cannot immolate yourself to it. Love comes into being only when the self is absent; and as long as you are seeking gratification, escapes, refusing to understand your confusion in relationship, you are merely emphasizing the self, and therefore denying love.

Banaras, 2nd Public Talk, January 23, 1949
Collected Works, Vol. V, p. 194

The moment I am conscious that I love, self-activity has come into being; therefore, it ceases to be love.

Now, our question surely is: Is it possible for the mind to experience, to have that state, not momentarily, not at rare moments, but—I would not use the word *everlasting* or *forever,* because that would imply time—to have that state, to be in that state without regard to time? Surely, that is an important discovery to be made by each one of us because that is the door to love; all other doors are activities of the self. Where there is action of the self, there is no love—love is not of time. You can't practice love. If you do, then it is a self-conscious activity of the 'me' which hopes through living to gain a result.

So, love is not of time; you can't come upon it through any conscious effort, through any discipline, through identification, which are all a process of time. The mind, knowing only the process of time, cannot recognize love. Love is the only thing that is new, eternally new. Since most of us have cultivated the mind, which is a process of time, which is the result of time, we do not know what love is. We talk about love; we say we love people, love our children, our wives, our neighbor; we say we love nature; but the moment I am conscious that I love, self-activity has come into being; therefore, it ceases to be love.

This total process of the mind is to be understood only through relationship—relationship with nature, with people, with our own projection, with everything. In fact, life is nothing but relationship. Though we may attempt to isolate ourselves from relationship, we cannot exist without relationship; though relationship is pain from which we try to run away through isolation by becoming a hermit and so on, we cannot do that. All these methods are an indication of the activity of the self. Seeing this whole picture, being aware of this whole process of time as consciousness, without any choice, without any determined, purposive intention, without the desire for any result, you will see that this process of time comes to an end voluntarily, not induced, not as a result of desire. It is only when that process comes to an end, that love is, which is eternally new.

Madras, 12th Public Talk, February 10, 1952
Collected Works, Vol. VI, pp. 322-3

When you love, there is neither the 'you' nor the 'me'.

It is only when the mind is quiet that it shall know love, and that state of quietness is not a thing to be cultivated. Cultivation is still the action of the mind, discipline is still a product of the mind, and a mind that is disciplined, controlled, subjugated, a mind that is resisting, explaining, cannot know love. You may read, you may listen to what is being said about love, but that is not love. Only when you put away the things of the mind, only when your hearts are empty of the things of the mind, is there love. Then you will know what it is to love without separation, without distance, without time, without fear—and that is not reserved to the few. Love knows no hierarchy, there is only love. There are the many and the one, an exclusiveness, only when you do not love. When you love, Sir, there is neither the 'you' nor the 'me', in that state there is only a flame without smoke.

Bombay, 5th Public Talk, March 12, 1950
Collected Works, Vol. VI, p. 133

Can the mind come upon love without discipline, without thought, without enforcement, without any book, any teacher?

In this torn, desert world there is no love because pleasure and desire play the greatest roles. Yet, without love your daily life has no meaning. And you cannot have love if there is no beauty. Beauty is not something you see—not a beautiful tree, a beautiful picture, a beautiful building, or a beautiful woman. There is beauty only when your heart and mind know what love is. Without love and that sense of beauty there is no virtue, and you know very well that, do what you will—improve society, feed the poor—you will only be creating more mischief, for without love there is only ugliness and poverty in your own heart and mind. But, when there is love and beauty, whatever you do is right, whatever you do is in order. If you know how to love, then you can do what you like because it will solve all other problems.

So we reach the point: Can the mind come upon love without discipline, without thought, without enforcement, without any book, any teacher or leader—come upon it as one comes upon a lovely sunset?

It seems to me that one thing is absolutely necessary, and that is passion without motive—passion that is not the result of some commitment or attachment, passion that is not lust. A man who does not know what passion is will never know love because love can come into being only when there is total self-abandonment.

A mind that is seeking is not a passionate mind, and to come upon love without seeking it is the only way to find it—to come upon it unknowingly and not as the result of any effort or experience. Such a love, you will find, is not of time; such a love is both personal and impersonal, is both the one and the many. Like a flower that has perfume you can smell it or pass it by. That flower is for everybody and for the one who takes trouble to breathe it deeply and look at it with delight. Whether one is very near in the garden, or very far away, it is the same to the flower because it is full of that perfume, and therefore it is sharing with everybody.

Love is something that is new, fresh, alive. It has no yesterday and no tomorrow. It is beyond the turmoil of thought. It is only the innocent mind which knows what love is, and the innocent mind can live in the world which is not innocent. To find this extraordinary thing which man has sought endlessly through sacrifice, through worship, through relationship, through sex, through every form of pleasure and pain, is only possible when thought comes to understand itself and comes naturally to an end. Then love has no opposite, then love has no conflict.

You may ask: "If I find such a love, what happens to my wife, my children, my family? They must have security." When you put such a question you have never been outside the field of thought, the field of consciousness. When once you have been outside that field you will never ask such a question because then you will know what love is, in which there is no thought and therefore no time. You may read this mesmerized and enchanted, but actually to go beyond thought and time—which means going beyond sorrow—is to be aware that there is a different dimension called *love*.

But you don't know how to come to this extraordinary fount—so what do you do? If you don't know what to do, you do nothing, don't you? Absolutely nothing. Then, inwardly you are completely silent. Do you understand what that means? It means that you are not seeking, not wanting, not pursuing; there is no center at all. Then there is love.

Freedom from the Known, pp. 86-7

Is there an approach to the fact without a single motive?

Let us go into the question of what intelligent relationship is—not the relationship of thought with its image. Our brains are mechanical—mechanical in the sense that they are repetitive, never free, struggling within the same field, thinking they are free by moving from one corner to the other in the same field, which is choice, and thinking that choice is freedom, which is merely the same thing. One's brain, which has evolved through ages of time, through tradition, through education, through conformity, through adjustment, has become mechanical. There may be parts of one's brain which are free but one does not know, so do not assert that. Do not say: "Yes, there is part of me that is free"; that is meaningless. The fact remains that the brain has become mechanical, traditional, repetitive, and that it has its own cunningness, its own capacity to adjustment, to discern; but it is always within a limited area and is fragmented. Thought has its home in the physical cells of the brain.

The brain has become mechanical, as is exemplified when I say, "I am a Christian," or, "I am not a Christian; I am a Hindu; I believe; I have faith; I do not have faith"—it is all a mechanical, repetitive process, reaction to another reaction, and so on. The human brain, being conditioned, has its own artificial, mechanical intelligence like a computer. We will keep that expression—*mechanical intelligence.* (Billions and billions of dollars are being spent to find out if a computer can operate exactly like the brain.) Thought, which is born of memory, knowledge, stored in the brain, is mechanical; it may have the capacity to invent, but it is still mechanical—invention is totally different from creation. Thought is trying to discover a different way of life, or a different social order. But any discovery of a social order by thought is still within the field of confusion. We are asking: Is there an intelligence which has no cause and which can act in our relationships? Not the mechanical state of relationship which exists now.

Our relationships are mechanical. One has certain biological urges and one fulfills them. One demands certain comforts, certain companionship because one is lonely or depressed and, by holding on to another, perhaps that depression will disappear. But in one's relationships with another, intimate or otherwise, there is always a cause, a motive, a ground from which one establishes a relationship—that is mechanical. It has been happening for millennia; there appears always to have been a conflict between woman and man, a constant battle, each pursuing his or her own line, never meeting, like two railway lines. This relationship is always limited because it is from the activity of thought which itself is limited.

Wherever there is limitation there must be conflict. In any form of association—one belongs to this group and another belongs to another group—there is solitude, isolation; where there is isolation there must be conflict. This is a law, not invented by the speaker, it is obviously so. Thought is ever in limitation and therefore isolating itself. Therefore, in relationship, where there is the activity of thought there must be conflict. See the reality of it. See the actuality of this fact, not as an idea, but as something that is happening in one's active daily life—divorces, quarrels, hating each other, jealousy; you know the misery of it all. The wife wants to hurt you, is jealous of you, and you are jealous—which are all mechanical reactions, the repetitive activity of thought in relationship, bringing conflict. That is a fact.

Now, how do you deal with that fact? Here is a fact: your wife and you quarrel. She hates you, and also there is your mechanical response, you hate. You discover that it is the remembrance of things that have happened stored in the brain, continuing day after day. Your whole thinking is a process of isolation—and she also is in isolation. Neither of you ever discovers the truth of the isolation. Now, how do you look at that fact? What are you to do with that fact? What is your response? Do you face this fact with a motive, a cause? Be careful, do not say, "My wife hates me," and smother it over—although you also hate her, dislike her, don't want to be with her, because you are both isolated. You are ambitious for one thing, she is ambitious for something else. So, your relationship operates in isolation. Do you approach the fact with reason, with a ground, which are all motives? Or, do you approach it without a motive, without cause? When you approach it without a cause, what then happens? Watch it. Please do not jump to some conclusion; watch it in yourself. Previously you have approached this problem mechanically with a motive, with some reason, a ground from which you act. Now you see the foolishness of such an action because it is the result of thought.

So, is there an approach to the fact without a single motive? That is, you have no motive, yet she may have a motive. Then, if you have no motive, how are you looking at the fact? The fact is not different from you: you *are* the fact. You are ambition, you are hate, you depend on somebody—you are that. There is an observation of the fact, which is yourself, without any kind of reason, motive. Is that possible? If you do not do that, you live perpetually in conflict. And you may say that that is the way of life. If you accept that as the way of life, that is your business, your pleasure. Your brain, tradition and habit, tell you that it is inevitable. But when you see the absurdity of such acceptance, then you are bound to see that all this travail is you yourself; *you* are the enemy, not her. You have met the enemy and discovered it is yourself.

So, can you observe this whole movement of 'me', the self, and the traditional acceptance that you are separate? Which becomes foolish when you examine the whole field of the consciousness of humanity. You have come to a point in understanding what intelligence is. We said that intelligence is without a cause, as love is without a cause. If love has a cause, it is not love, obviously. If you are *intelligent* so that the government employs you, or *intelligent* because you are following me, that is not intelligence, that is capacity. Intelligence has no cause. Therefore, see if you are looking at yourself with a cause. Are you looking at this fact: that you are thinking, working, feeling in isolation, and that isolation must inevitably breed everlasting conflict? That isolation is yourself; you are the enemy. When you look at yourself without a motive, is there 'self'?—self as the cause and the effect, self as the result of time, which is the movement from cause to effect? When you look at yourself, look at this fact—without a cause—there is the ending of something and the beginning of something totally new.

Saanen, Switzerland, July 15, 1982
The Flame of Attention, pp. 98-101

IX. To Be Related Means the Ending of the 'Me'

I often wonder why we go to meetings to listen to others, why we want to talk things over together, and indeed, why we have problems at all. Human beings throughout the world seem to have so many, such multiple problems. And we go to meetings, like these, hoping to pick up some kind of idea, a formula, a way of life, that might perhaps be of some use or help us to overcome our many difficulties, the complex problem of living. And yet, although man has lived for millions of years, he is still struggling, always groping after something such as happiness or reality or a mind that is not disturbed, that can live in this world frankly, happily, sanely. And yet, strangely, we don't seem to come upon any of these realities that will be totally, lastingly satisfying. And now here we are for the fourth time, and I wonder why we meet or talk to each other at all? There has been so much propaganda, so many people have said how we should live, what we should do, what we should think; they have invented many theories—what the State should do, what society must be; and the theologians throughout the world state a fixed dogma or belief around which they build fantastic myths and theories. And through propaganda, the endless pouring out of words, we are shaped, our minds are conditioned and gradually we lose all feeling.

To us, intellect is enormously important, thought is essential—thought which can operate logically, sanely, intelligently. But I wonder if thought has any place in relationship at all? Because that is what we are going to talk over together this evening. We said we must ask fundamental questions, essential questions. The last three times that we met here, we faced that enormous question to which man has been seeking an answer: what is the relationship of man, who is caught in this turmoil, in this endless misery (with a fluttering of occasional happiness), what is his relationship to that immense reality—if a relationship does exist at all? We went into that.

Perhaps this evening we may consider, not intellectually, but actually—with our hearts, our minds, our whole being—we may succeed in giving complete attention to this question of man's relationship to man, and not only his relationship with another, but also his relationship to nature, to the universe, to every living thing. But, as we saw, society is making us and we are making ourselves more and more mechanical, superficial, callous, indifferent—slaughter is going on in the Far East, and we are comparatively undisturbed. We have become very prosperous, but that very prosperity is destroying us because we are becoming indifferent and lazy, because we are becoming mechanical, superficial, and we are losing close relationship to all men, to all living things. And it seems to me that it is very important to ask this question: What is relationship, whether there is any relationship at all, and what place in that relationship love and thought and pleasure have?

As we said, we are going to consider this question, but not intellectually, because that means fragmentarily. We have broken up life into the intellect and the emotions, we have departmentalized our whole existence, with the specialist in the field of science, the artist, the writer, the priest, and the ordinary laymen such as you and me! We are broken up into nationalities, into classes, divisions which grow wider and deeper. Let us consider this question of relationship, which is really extraordinarily important, because to live is to be related; and in considering this question of relationship we shall ask what it means to live.

What is our life, which needs deep relationship with another, whether as wife, husband, children, family, community, or any other unit? In considering it we cannot possibly deal with this question in fragments, because if we take one section, one part of the totality of existence and try to solve that one part, then there is no way out of it at all. But perhaps we shall be able to understand and live differently if we can deal with this question of relationship totally, not in fragments—not as the individual and the community, and the individual opposing the community, the individual and society, the individual and religion, and so on—as these are all fragmentations; they are all broken up. We are always trying to solve our problems by understanding a little fragment of this whole business of existence.

So could we, at least for this evening, and I hope also for the rest of our lives, look at life not in fragments—as a Catholic, a Protestant, a specialist in Zen, or following a particular guru, Master—which is all so absurdly childish. We have got an immense problem, that is, to understand existence, to understand how to live. And, as we said, living is relationship; there is no living if we are not related. And most of us, not being related in the deeper sense of that word, we try to identify ourselves with something—with the nation, with a particular system, or philosophy, or a particular dogma or belief. That's what is going on throughout the world: the identification of each individual with something—with the family, or with oneself. And I don't know what it means to "identify with oneself."

This fragmentary, separative existence inevitably leads to various forms of violence. So, if we could give our attention to this question of relationship, then we could perhaps solve the social inequalities, injustices, immorality, and that terrifying thing *respectability,* which man has cultivated; to be respectable is to be moral according to that which is really essentially immoral.

So, is there any relationship at all? Relationship implies being in contact, in touch, deeply, fundamentally, with nature, with another human being—to be related, not in blood, or as part of the family, or as husband and wife, as these are hardly relationships at all. To find out the nature of this question, we must look at another issue, which is this whole mechanism of building images, putting them together, creating an idea, a symbol, in which man lives. Most of us have images about ourselves—what we think we are, what we should be, the image of oneself and the image of another; we have these images in relationship. You have the image about the speaker, and as the speaker doesn't know you he has no image. But if you know somebody very intimately you have already built an image, that very intimacy implies the image that you have about that person—the wife has an image about the husband and the husband has an image about her. Then there is the image of society and the images that one has about God, about truth, about *everything.*

How does this image come into being? And if it is there, as it is with practically everybody, then how can there be any real relationship? Relationship implies being in contact with each other deeply, profoundly. Out of that deep relationship there can be co-operation, working together, doing things together. But if there is an image—I have an image about you and you have an image about me—what relationship can exist, except the relationship of an idea, or a symbol, or a certain memory, which becomes the image. Do these images have relationships, and is that perhaps what relationship is? Can there be love in the real sense of that word—not according to the priests, or according to the theologians, or according to the communist, or this or that person, but actually the quality of that feeling of love—when the relationship is merely conceptual, imaginative, not factual? There can only be a relationship between human beings when we accept *what is,* not *what should be.* We are always living in the world of formulas, concepts, which are the images of thought. So, can thought, can intellect bring about right relationship? Can the mind, the brain, with all its self-protective instruments built up through millions of years—can that brain, which is the whole response of memory and thought, bring about right relationship between human beings? What place has the image, thought, in relationship? Has it any place at all?

I wonder if you ask these questions of yourself when you look at those chestnut trees with their blooms like white candles against the blue sky. What relationship exists between you and that, what relationship have you actually got—not emotionally, nor sentimentally, what is your relationship with such things? And, if you have lost the relationship with these things in nature, how can you be related to man? The more we live in towns, the less do we have any relation with nature. You go out for a walk on a Sunday and look at the trees and say, "How lovely," and go back to your life of routine, living in a series of drawers, which are called houses, flats. You are losing relationship with nature. You can see this by the fact that you go to museums and you spend a whole morning looking at pictures, abstractions of *what is,* and this shows that you have really totally lost your contact, your relationship with nature: pictures, concerts, statues, have all become terribly important and you never look at the tree, the bird, the marvelous lighting of a cloud.

Now, what is relationship? Have we any relationship with another at all? Are we so enclosed, self-protected that our relationship has become merely superficial, sensual, pleasurable? Because, after all, if we examine ourselves very deeply and very quietly—not according to Freud or Jung or some other expert, but actually look at ourselves as we are—then perhaps we can find out how we isolate ourselves daily, how we build around ourselves a wall of resistance, of fear. To *look* at ourselves is more important and much more fundamental than to look at ourselves according to specialists.

If you look at yourself according to Jung or Freud or the Buddha, or somebody else, you are looking through the eyes of another. And you are doing that all the time; we have no eyes of our own to look and therefore we lose the beauty of the *look*.

So, when you look at yourselves directly, don't you find that your daily activities—your thought, your ambitions, your demands, your aggressions, the constant longing to be loved and to love, the constant gnawing of fear, the agony of isolation—don't these all make for extraordinary separativeness and fundamental isolation? And when there is that deep isolation, how can you be related to somebody else, to that other person who is also isolating himself, through his ambition, greed, avarice, demand for domination, possession, power, and all the rest of it? So, there are these two entities called human beings, living in their own isolation and breeding children and so on, but all this is isolation. And co-operation between these two isolated entities becomes mechanical; they must have some co-operation to live at all, to have a family, to go to the office or factory and work there, but they always remain isolated entities, with their beliefs and dogmas, their nationalities . . . you know all the screens that man has built around himself to separate himself from others. So, that isolation is essentially the factor of not being related. And in that isolated so-called relationship, pleasure becomes most important.

In the world you can see how pleasure is becoming more and more demanding, insistent, because all pleasure, if you observe carefully, is a process of isolation; and one has to consider this question of pleasure in the context of relationship. Pleasure is the product of thought—isn't it? Pleasure was in the thing which you experienced yesterday, the beauty or the sensuous perception, or sexual sensuous excitement; you think about it, you build an image of that pleasure which you experienced yesterday. And so thought sustains, gives nourishment, to that thing which was called pleasurable yesterday. And so thought demands the continuity of that pleasure today. The more you think about that experience that you had, which gave you a delight at the moment, the more thought gives it a continuity as pleasure and desire. And what relationship has this to the fundamental question of human existence, which concerns how we are related? If our relationship is the outcome of sexual pleasure, or the pleasure of the family, of ownership, domination, control, the fear of not being protected, not having inward security and therefore always seeking pleasure—then what place has pleasure in relationship? The demand for pleasure does destroy all relationship, whether it be sexual or of any other kind. And if we observe clearly, all our so called moral values are based on pleasure, though we put it over with the righteous sounding morality of our respectable society.

So, when we ask ourselves, when we look at ourselves, deeply, we see this activity of self-isolation, the 'me', the 'I', the 'ego', building resistance round itself and that very resistance *is* the 'me'. That is isolation, that is what creates fragments, the fragmentary look of the thinker and the thought. So, what place has pleasure—which is the outcome of a memory given sustenance and nourishment by thought, thought which is always old, which is never free—what has that thought, which has centered its existence in pleasure, to do with relationship? Do please ask yourselves this question, don't merely listen to the speaker—he is gone tomorrow and you have to live your own life. So the speaker is of no importance whatsoever; what is important is to ask these questions of yourself. And, to ask such questions you have to be terribly serious, you have to be completely dedicated to the search, because it is only when you are serious that you live, it's only when you are deeply, fundamentally, earnest that life opens, has meaning, has beauty. You have to ask this question: whether it is not a fact that you live in an image, in a formula, in an isolating fragment. Is it not out of that isolation that fear—with its pain and pleasure, the outcome of thought—has become aware of this isolation? That image then tries to identify itself with something permanent: God, truth, the nation, the flag, and the rest of it.

So, if thought is old—and it is always old and therefore never free—how can thought understand relationship? Relationship is always in the present, in the living present, not in the dead past of memory, of remembrances of pleasure and pain; relationship is active *now*. To be related means just that. When you look at somebody with eyes that are full of affection, love, there is immediate relationship. When you can look at a cloud with eyes that are seeing for the first time, then there is deep relationship. But if thought comes in, then that relationship belongs to the image. So then one asks: what is love? Is love pleasure? Is love desire? Is love a memory of the many things that have been built up, stored up, with regard to your wife, to your husband, to your neighbor, the society, the community, with your God—can that be said to be love?

If love is the product of thought, as it is with most people, then that love is hedged about, caught in the network of jealousy, of envy, the desire to dominate, to possess and be possessed, this longing to be loved and to love. In that, can there be love for the one and for the many? If I love one, do I destroy the love of the other? And, as with most of us love is pleasure, companionship, comfort, the seclusion and the sense of being protected in the family, is there really any love? Can a man who is bound to his family love his neighbor? You may talk about love theoretically, go to church and love God—whatever that may mean—and the next day go to the office and destroy your neighbor, because you are competing with him and want his job, his possessions, and you want to better yourself, comparing yourself with him. So, when all this activity is going on inside you, morning till night, even when you are asleep through your dreams, can you be related? Or, is relationship something entirely different?

Relationship can only exist when there is total abandonment of the self, the 'me'. When the 'me' is not, then you are related; in that there is no separation whatsoever. Probably one has not felt that, the total denial—not intellectually, but actually—the total cessation of the 'me'. And perhaps that's what most of us are seeking, sexually or through identification with something greater. But that again, that process of identification with something greater is the product of thought; and thought is old—like the 'me', the ego, the 'I'—it is of yesterday, it is always old. The question then arises: How is it possible to let go this isolating process completely, this process which is centered in the 'me'. How is this to be done? You understand the question? How am I—whose every activity of everyday life is of fear, anxiety, despair, sorrow, confusion, and hope—how is the 'me' which separates itself from another—through identification with God, with its conditioning, with its society, with its social and moral activity, with the State, and so on—how is that to die, to disappear, so that the human being can be related? Because, if we are not related, then we are going to live at war with each other. There may be no killing of each other, because that is becoming too dangerous, except in far away countries. How can we live so that there is no separation, so that we really can cooperate?

There is so much to do in the world: to wipe away poverty, to live happily, to live with delight instead of with agony and fear, to build a totally different kind of society, a morality which is above all morality. But this can only be when all the morality of present-day society is totally denied. There is so much to do, and it cannot be done if there is this constant isolating process going on. We speak of the 'me' and the 'mine', and the 'other'—the other is beyond the wall, the 'me' and 'mine' is this side of the wall. So, how can that essence of resistance, which is the 'me', how can that be completely let go? Because that is really the most fundamental question in all relationship, as one sees that the relationship between images is not relationship at all and that when that kind of relationship exists there must be conflict, that we must be at each other's throats.

When you put yourself that question, inevitably you'll say: "Must I live in a vacuum, in a state of emptiness?" I wonder if you have ever known what it is to have a mind that is completely empty. You have lived in space that is created by the 'me'—which is a very small space. The space which the 'I', the self-isolating process, has built between one person and another, that is all the space we know—the space between itself and the circumference—the frontier which thought has built. And in this space we live, in this space there is division. You say: "If I let myself go, or if I abandon the center of 'me', I will live in a vacuum." But have you ever really let go the 'me', actually, so that there is no 'me' at all? Have you ever lived in this world, gone to the office in that spirit, lived with your wife or with your husband? If you have lived that way you will know that there is a state of relationship in which the 'me' is not, which is not Utopia, which is not a thing dreamt about, or a mystical, nonsensical experience, but something that can be actually done—to live at a dimension where there is relationship with all human beings.

But that can only be when we understand what love is. And to be, to live in that state, one must understand the pleasure of thought and all its mechanism. Then all complicated mechanism that one has built for oneself, around oneself, can be seen at a glance—one hasn't got to go through all this analytical process point by point. All analysis is fragmentary, and therefore there is no answer through that door.

There is this immense complex problem of existence, with all its fears, anxieties, hopes, fleeting happiness, and joys, but analysis is not going to solve it. What will do so, is to take it all in swiftly, as a whole. You know, you understand something only when you look—not with a prolonged, trained look, the trained look of an artist, a scientist, or the man who has practised how to look—but you see it if you look at it with complete attention, you see the whole thing in one glance. And then you will see you are out of it; then you are out of time. Time has a stop and sorrow therefore ends. A man that is in sorrow or fear is not related. How can a man who is pursuing power have relationship? He may have a family, sleep with his wife, but he is not related. A man who is competing with another has no relationship at all. And all our social structure, with its un-morality, is based on this. To be fundamentally, essentially related means the ending of the 'me' that breeds separation and sorrow.

Paris, April 25, 1968
Talks in Europe 1968, pp. 78-88

Bibliography

The Collected Works of J. Krishnamurti, first published by Kendall/Hunt, 1991-1992. Copyright © KFA 1991/1992.

Vol. I (1933-34) *The Art of Listening*
Vol. II (1934-35) *What Is Right Action?*
Vol. III (1936-44) *The Mirror of Relationship*
Vol. IV (1945-48) *The Observer Is the Observed*
Vol. V (1948-49) *Choiceless Awareness*
Vol. VI (1949-52) *The Origin of Conflict*
Vol. VII (1952-53) *Tradition and Creativity*
Vol. VIII (1953-55) *What Are You Seeking?*
Vol. IX (1955-56) *The Answer Is in the Problem*
Vol. X (1956-57) *A Light to Yourself*
Vol. XI (1958-60) *Crisis in Consciousness*
Vol. XII (1961) *There Is No Thinker, Only Thought*
Vol. XIII (1962-63) *A Psychological Revolution*
Vol. XIV (1963-64) *The New Mind*
Vol. XV (1964-65) *The Dignity of Living*
Vol. XVI (1965-66) *The Beauty of Death*
Vol. XVII (1966-67) *Perennial Questions*

Commentaries on Living, Series I, II, III, Quest Books, 1967. Copyright © KFA, 1956.

Conversations, Krishnamurti Foundation Trust, 1970. Copyright © KFT, 1970.

A Dialogue With Oneself, Krishnamurti Foundation Trust, 1977. Copyright © KFT, 1977.

Education and the Significance of Life, Harper & Row, 1981. Copyright © KFA, 1953.

The First and Last Freedom, HarperSanFrancisco, 1975.
Copyright © KFA, 1954.

The Flame of Attention, Harper & Row, 1984.
Copyright © KFT, 1983.

Freedom From the Known, Harper & Row, 1969.
Copyright © KFT, 1969.

Meeting Life, HarperSanFrancisco, 1991.
Copyright © KFT, 1991.

Mind Without Measure, Krishnamurti Foundation India, 1990.
Copyright © KFT, 1983.

The Network of Thought, Harper & Row, 1982.
Copyright © KFT, 1982.

On Relationship, HarperSanFrancisco, 1992.
Copyright © KFT, 1992.

Questions and Answers, Mirananda, 1982.
Copyright © KFT, 1982.

The Second Penguin Krishnamurti Reader, Penguin, 1986.
Copyright © KFT, 1970, 1971.

Talks in Europe 1968, Servire, 1969.
Copyright © KFT, 1969.

Think on These Things, HarperPerennial, 1989.
Copyright © KFA, 1964.

The Wholeness of Life, Harper & Row, 1981.
Copyright © KFT, 1979.

THE COLLECTED WORKS OF J. KRISHNAMURTI

(18 Volumes)

ISBN : 978-81-208-3090-5 (Set)
Rs. 350 (each volume)

The Art of Listening	Volume 1	(1933-1934)
What is Right Action?	Volume 2	(1934-1935)
The Mirror of Relationship	Volume 3	(1936-1944)
The Observer Is the Observed	Volume 4	(1945-1948)
Choiceless Awareness	Volume 5	(1948-1949)
The Origin of Conflict	Volume 6	(1949-1952)
Tradition and Creativity	Volume 7	(1952-1953)
What Are You Seeking?	Volume 8	(1953-1955)
The Answer Is in the Problem	Volume 9	(1955-1956)
A Light to Yourself	Volume 10	(1956-1957)
Crisis in Consciousness	Volume 11	(1958-1960)
There Is No Thinker, Only Thought	Volume 12	(1961)
A Psychological Revolution	Volume 13	(1962-1963)
The New Mind	Volume 14	(1963-1964)
The Dignity of Living	Volume 15	(1964-1965)
The Beauty of Death	Volume 16	(1965-1966)
Perennial Questions	Volume 17	(1966-1967)
The Concordance Index	Volume 18	(Index for Vols 1-17)

Published by :

MOTILAL BANARSIDASS PUBLISHERS
PRIVATE LIMITED • DELHI

For further information about Krishnamurti Libraries, Retreats, Study Centers, Schools and events worldwide, as well as other publications, please contact the following:

Krishnamurti Foundation of America
P.O. Box 1560
Ojai, California 93024 U.S.A.
E-mail: kfa@kfa.org
www.kfa.org

Krishnamurti Foundation Trust, Ltd.
Brockwood Park
Bramdean, Hampshire
England SO24 0LQ
E-mail: info@brockwood.org.uk
www.brockwood.org.uk

Krishnamurti Foundation India
64-65 Greenways Road
Vasanta Vihar
Chennai
India 600 028
E-mail: kfihq@vsnl.com
www.kfionline.org

Also visit the website
jkrishnamurti.org